Mindset Evolution:
Building Your Mind for the Modern World

MELISSA HANKINS

Thank You

To my sons, Mason and Benjamin, who fill my life with joy and remind me daily of what matters most. You're the inspiration behind all that I do.

To my partner, Dairrick, whose unwavering support and encouragement made this book possible. You bring light and purpose to each day, showing me the deepest meanings of love and growth.

To my mom, Lynn, who embodies resilience and showed me how strength grows through life's challenges.

In loving memory of Alexander Scott Hankins, whose precious soul opened my heart to motherhood and changed my life forever, and Marcus Alexander Hankins, who gave me the universe in the form of three incredible sons.

To my closest friends, who listened deeply, offered wisdom freely, and walked alongside me on this journey of growth.

Finally, to you, the reader. Your commitment to growth gives purpose to these words. Thank you for joining me on this journey of **Mindset Evolution**.

MINDSET EVOLUTION

Disclaimer and Legal Notes

This book is intended for educational and informational purposes only, based on the author's personal experiences, research, and insights into mindfulness, personal growth, and navigating modern challenges. It is not a substitute for professional medical, psychological, or mental health advice, diagnosis, or treatment. Readers with specific concerns are encouraged to consult qualified professionals.

The practices and strategies outlined herein are designed for general personal development. Individual results may vary, and the author does not guarantee specific outcomes. While every effort has been made to ensure the accuracy and reliability of the content, the author is not responsible for errors, omissions, or the consequences of implementing the ideas discussed in this book.

The examples and scenarios used are illustrative and do not depict specific individuals or events. Any resemblance to actual persons or situations is purely coincidental.

All rights reserved. No part of this book may be reproduced, distributed, or transmitted in any form or by any means, including photocopying, recording, or other electronic or mechanical methods, without the prior written permission of the author, except for brief quotations used in reviews or discussions.

Self-Published by the Author
© 2024 BraverForTomorrow.com

Table of Contents

Introduction:
Navigating the New Frontier of Human Potential 1

Chapter 1:
Understanding the Mind in the Digital Age 4

Chapter 2:
Mindfulness in the Modern World..20

Chapter 3:
Cultivating Resilience and Adaptability in Uncertain Times...37

Chapter 4:
Harnessing Creativity and Imagination for Personal Growth .52

Chapter 5:
Unlocking the Power of the Subconscious Mind 66

Chapter 6:
Expanding Cultural and Philosophical Horizons 77

Chapter 7:
Mastering Modern Complexity 88

Chapter 8:
Sustaining Lifelong Growth and Adaptation......................100

Conclusion:
The Ever-Evolving Journey 111

This page intentionally left blank

Introduction: Navigating the New Frontier of Human Potential

We live in an era of unprecedented change and possibility. Artificial intelligence is reshaping our world, global challenges are growing more complex, and the pace of innovation continues to accelerate. In this landscape of constant transformation, one truth becomes increasingly clear, our ability to grow and adapt while staying true to ourselves, is the difference between thriving and merely surviving.

Traditional approaches to personal development, while valuable in their time, are no longer sufficient for today's challenges. Our rapidly changing world demands new tools and strategies for growth. We need strategies that integrate modern research with traditional wisdom, that help us partner with technology while preserving our humanity, and that prepare us for a future arriving faster than ever before.

This is where **Mindset Evolution** enters the conversation. Our capacity for growth and adaptation extends throughout life. Our ability to develop new capabilities, strengthen emotional intelligence, and enhance resilience isn't fixed, it's a potential we can actively cultivate through understanding and practice. However, knowing this potential exists isn't enough, we need practical strategies to activate it.

Throughout this book, you'll discover how to navigate the complexities of modern life while developing the mental capabilities required for success. We'll explore:

- How to create conditions for lasting personal transformation
- Ways to partner with technology while maintaining human connection
- Techniques for cultivating mindful awareness in a distraction filled world
- Strategies for building resilience in times of change
- Methods for enhancing creativity alongside artificial intelligence
- Approaches to working with your deeper patterns of thinking and behavior
- Frameworks for understanding and navigating complexity
- Tools for sustainable, lifelong development

What sets this book apart is its integration of diverse perspectives and proven approaches. By combining current research with traditional wisdom, technological understanding with human insight, and individual practice with collective learning, we create a comprehensive toolkit for modern development. This multifaceted approach ensures you're equipped with practical strategies that work in real world situations.

Each chapter serves as both a guide and practical toolkit, combining research-based insights with actionable strategies. You'll find carefully crafted exercises tested in real situations, clear step-by-step practices for building new capabilities, and real-world applications that show these principles in action. The concepts build progressively, creating a thorough framework for understanding and developing your mind in ways that adapt to your evolving needs.

This isn't a book to read passively, it's an invitation to embark on a transformative journey, one that will challenge your assumptions, expand your capabilities, and help you develop the mindset needed to thrive in our rapidly evolving world. I encourage you to engage actively with the practices rather than simply reading about them. Try them out, modify them for your needs, and note which approaches resonate most strongly with you. The goal isn't to implement everything at once, but to build a personalized toolkit that works for your unique situation.

As we stand at this crucial juncture in human history, the ability to consciously evolve our mindset isn't just beneficial, it's essential. Whether you're a leader guiding others through change, a professional navigating shifting landscapes, or someone committed to personal growth, this book provides the understanding and tools needed to thrive in our modern world.

Are you ready to begin? Turn the page, and let's explore the new frontier of human potential together.

Chapter 1: Understanding the Mind in the Digital Age

Our mindset influences how we interpret and respond to life, how we face challenges, embrace opportunities, and navigate an ever-changing world. As our world becomes increasingly digital and interconnected, understanding and cultivating our mindset has become more crucial than ever. Today, thanks to advancements in neuroscience and brain imaging technologies, we have unprecedented insights into how our thoughts and beliefs shape our brains, and how this process is both challenged and enhanced by our digital environment.

The Neuroscience of Mindset

At the heart of modern mindset theory lies the concept of neuroplasticity, the brain's remarkable ability to reorganize itself by forming new neural connections throughout life. This understanding has revolutionary implications, our brains are not fixed entities, but highly adaptable organs that can be reshaped through our experiences, thoughts, and focused effort, even in the face of constant digital stimulation.

Dr. Carol Dweck's research at Stanford University has been instrumental in understanding how mindset affects learning and development. Her studies, published in journals including *Psychological Science*, have demonstrated a crucial distinction, people who believe their abilities can be developed (a growth mindset), consistently achieve higher levels of success and learning compared to those who view their abilities as unchangeable (a fixed mindset). This research has helped establish the profound connection between our beliefs about our capabilities and our actual capacity for growth and adaptation.

Dr. Dweck's research demonstrates that students with a growth mindset approach learning more positively, show greater resilience in the face of challenges, and achieve better academic outcomes. Building on this foundation, neuroimaging research by Dr. Jason Moser and colleagues revealed that individuals with a growth mindset show distinctive neural activity patterns when processing mistakes, suggesting that our beliefs about learning and ability influence not just our behavior, but our brain's response to challenges.

This understanding becomes particularly relevant as we navigate our increasingly digital world. Building on these fundamental insights about growth mindset, researchers have identified several distinct mindset dimensions that shape how we adapt and thrive in today's environment:

1. Resilience Mindset: The belief in one's ability to bounce back from adversity, particularly important in navigating the constant changes of the digital landscape. This mindset helps us view technological disruptions as opportunities rather than threats.

2. Abundance Mindset: The belief that there are enough resources and opportunities for everyone, helping to counter the scarcity mentality often triggered by social media comparison. This perspective enables healthier engagement with digital platforms.

3. Learning Mindset: A passion for learning and the belief that abilities can be developed, essential for thriving in an era of rapid technological change.

This mindset drives continuous adaptation and growth.

4. Possibility Mindset: The ability to see potential and opportunities where others see obstacles, crucial for innovation in the digital age. This perspective helps us harness technology creatively rather than feeling overwhelmed by it.

5. Mindfulness Mindset: The practice of present moment awareness and non-judgmental observation, particularly valuable in an age of constant digital distraction. This mindset helps us maintain focus and clarity amid information overload.

These mindsets work together as an integrated system for navigating our digital world. Just as Dr. Dweck's research shows how growth mindset changes neural activity patterns when processing challenges, each of these mindset dimensions influences how our brains respond to digital age demands. Through regular practice, these patterns of thinking become stronger, enhancing our ability to stay resilient, maintain perspective, continue learning, recognize opportunities, and remain present amid constant change. The neural adaptability demonstrated in Dr. Moser's research suggests that we can actively cultivate these mindsets, strengthening our capacity to thrive in our rapidly evolving environment.

Information Overload

Understanding how our brains respond to stress and overwhelm becomes particularly crucial as we face one of the defining challenges of our digital age, managing an unprecedented volume of information. From social media feeds and news alerts to work communications and entertainment options, we're confronted with a constant stream of data demanding our attention. This relentless influx of information can lead to what psychologists call "cognitive overload", a state where our mental resources are so taxed that our ability to process information and make decisions becomes impaired.

Dr. Daniel Levitin, neuroscientist and author of *The Organized Mind*, has extensively studied how information overload affects our brain function. His research shows that the daily deluge of information exhausts our neural resources, compromising not just our ability to process information, but also our capacity to make decisions and maintain emotional balance. Our brains evolved to process information in an environment vastly different from today's digital landscape, and constant information flows create unprecedented demands on our cognitive resources.

The manifestations of cognitive overload include:

1. Decision Fatigue: The natural decline in the quality of our decisions after making many choices throughout the day. Just as a muscle gets tired from overuse, our mental energy for decision-making becomes depleted, especially when faced with the constant choices our digital world demands.

2. Analysis Paralysis: A state where having access to too much information prevents us from taking action. Rather than helping us make better decisions, an overflow of data and opinions can leave us stuck in an endless loop of research and comparison.

3. Attention Fragmentation: The growing difficulty in maintaining sustained focus on single tasks, caused by frequent digital interruptions and our increasing habit of quickly switching between different activities. This scattered attention affects both our productivity and our ability to think deeply.

Understanding these cognitive challenges offers hope for managing them more effectively. Levitin's research suggests that by recognizing how our brains naturally process information, we can develop strategies that work with our cognitive architecture rather than against it.

Beyond the challenge of managing information volume, the way this information reaches and influences us, particularly through social media, presents unique challenges for our mental well-being and cognitive processing.

Social Media and Self Comparison

The rise of social media platforms has created new challenges for maintaining a healthy mindset. While these platforms offer unprecedented opportunities for connection and learning, they can also trigger intense social comparison and feelings of inadequacy.

The curated nature of social media can create what psychologists call "the highlight reel effect", where we compare our full life experience to others' carefully selected best moments. This phenomenon has particular implications for mindset development, as it can reinforce fixed mindset thinking and create barriers to authentic growth. Research shows that this constant exposure to curated content can affect our self-perception, stress levels, and how we evaluate our own progress and achievements.

Research from the Oxford Internet Institute reveals important distinctions in how different types of social media engagement affect wellbeing. Studies show that active engagement, such as having meaningful conversations, participating in community discussions, or sharing creative work, tends to have different psychological impacts than passive consumption like scrolling through feeds or repeatedly checking others' updates. When people use social media for purposeful connection and creation, they report greater satisfaction and less anxiety than those who primarily engage in passive viewing. Understanding social media as a tool for connection rather than a reflection of reality helps us harness its benefits while protecting ourselves from its potential psychological pitfalls.

The Attention Economy

In our digital age, attention has become perhaps our most valuable and contested resource. Tech companies employ increasingly sophisticated algorithms designed to capture and hold our attention, often at the expense of our well-being and productivity.

James Williams, a former Google strategist turned trained digital ethicist, argues that the "attention economy" represents one of the defining challenges of our time. In his research, he demonstrates how digital technologies systematically undermine human will and agency by commodifying our attention, leading us to spend time and mental energy in ways that often conflict with our deeper goals and values.

The implications of the attention economy extend beyond mere distraction. Research shows that repeated interruptions from notifications and task switching can create habitual patterns of scattered attention. Our brains adapt to these constant interruptions, making it increasingly difficult to maintain sustained focus on meaningful tasks.

The solution, Williams suggests, lies in reclaiming conscious control over our attention. This involves both personal practices and a broader understanding of how digital technologies are designed to influence our behavior. By developing this awareness, we can begin to make more intentional choices about how we engage with digital technology.

AI-Powered Personal Development

While conscious management of our attention remains crucial, emerging technologies also offer new possibilities for intentional growth. Artificial Intelligence is revolutionizing how we approach mindset development and personal growth. Through sophisticated data analysis and pattern recognition, AI-powered apps and platforms can now provide personalized guidance, tracking, and support in ways that were previously impossible. These technologies can identify individual learning patterns, track progress across multiple dimensions of development, and adjust strategies in real-time based on user responses and outcomes.

For example, AI-powered mental health applications can provide personalized support by analyzing interaction patterns, mood tracking, and behavioral data to offer tailored strategies for managing stress, anxiety, and negative thought patterns. Similarly, AI-enhanced coaching platforms combine artificial intelligence with human expertise to create more effective and accessible personal development experiences.

The key is to approach these tools as enhancers of human capability rather than replacements for human judgment. Success with AI-powered development tools comes when we use them to support our natural abilities while letting us stay in control of our growth. This balance allows us to harness the analytical power of AI while preserving the essential human elements of growth and development.

Virtual Reality and Immersive Learning

Virtual Reality (VR) is opening up new frontiers in experiential learning and mindset training. VR can create safe, controlled environments for practicing new skills, confronting fears, and cultivating positive mindsets.

Dr. Jeremy Bailenson, founding director of Stanford University's Virtual Human Interaction Lab, has demonstrated through his research how VR can fundamentally alter how people think and behave. His extensive studies show that immersive virtual experiences affect human psychology at a deep level, from reducing implicit racial bias through virtual embodiment experiences, to fostering environmental consciousness by letting people virtually experience the future consequences of present actions. Through what he terms "experience on demand," VR creates scenarios that would be impossible, dangerous, or prohibitively expensive in physical reality, allowing people to gain insights that can significantly impact their real-world behaviors and attitudes.

This technology is being used in increasingly sophisticated ways:

1. Therapeutic Purposes: Treating phobias and anxiety disorders through controlled exposure therapy. Patients can face their fears gradually in safe, customizable virtual environments, from fear of heights to public speaking anxiety.

2. Professional Development: Allowing the practice of complex skills in safe environments. Medical students can practice surgical procedures, pilots can handle emergency scenarios, and emergency responders can train for crisis situations without real-world risks.

3. Emotional Intelligence Training: Creating immersive empathy building experiences. Users can experience perspectives different from their own, helping them understand diverse viewpoints and develop deeper emotional awareness.

4. Cognitive Skill Development: Providing interactive environments for problem solving and decision-making. Users can practice complex scenarios repeatedly, receiving immediate feedback and adjusting their approaches.

5. Educational Settings: Creating experiential learning opportunities that would be impossible or impractical in physical classrooms. Students can explore historical events, conduct virtual science experiments, or visit remote locations.

Global Learning Communities

The internet has fundamentally transformed how we connect for learning and growth, creating unprecedented access to knowledge and expertise. Online platforms enable participation in global communities of practice, connecting learners with experts and peers across geographical and cultural boundaries. Research shows these digital learning environments can significantly enhance personal development when approached thoughtfully.

Global learning communities create unique pathways for mindset development through several mechanisms:

1. Inclusive Knowledge Sharing: Through these communities, learners gain access to previously restricted knowledge and expertise. Medical students can learn directly from leading researchers, aspiring entrepreneurs can engage with successful business leaders, and creative practitioners can study with master artists. This empowerment of knowledge creates opportunities for accelerated development that were impossible in traditional learning environments.

2. Cultural Intelligence Development: Regular interaction with diverse global perspectives enhances cultural understanding and adaptability. When engineers from different countries collaborate on technical challenges, they develop not just solutions but deeper appreciation for varied approaches to problem solving. Similarly, business professionals engaging in international project teams learn to navigate cultural differences while expanding their strategic thinking.

3. Collaborative Innovation: Global communities enable rapid iteration and improvement through collective intelligence. Software developers share code improvements in real-time, educators exchange teaching innovations across continents, and researchers build on each other's findings through immediate feedback. This accelerated collaboration creates learning opportunities that transcend traditional institutional boundaries.

4. Personalized Learning Pathways: Digital platforms can adapt to individual learning styles and goals while maintaining community connection. A designer might focus on user interface challenges while participating in a broader technology community, or a therapist might explore specific treatment modalities within a mental health network. This customization allows for focused development while benefiting from diverse perspectives.

5. Continuous Evolution: Unlike traditional learning environments with fixed schedules, global communities provide ongoing opportunities for growth and adaptation. Professionals can engage with emerging trends in real-time, test new approaches with immediate feedback, and continuously refine their understanding through active discussion and experimentation.

However, maximizing these benefits requires thoughtful engagement. Research shows the most successful participants in global learning communities develop clear strategies for:

- Establishing strong learning foundations through active participation and contribution

- Building meaningful relationships that extend beyond surface-level interactions
- Translating online insights into practical applications in local contexts
- Maintaining balanced engagement that supports rather than overwhelms personal development
- Creating structured approaches for implementing and testing new knowledge

Understanding these dynamics helps learners harness the transformative potential of global communities while avoiding common pitfalls, like information overwhelm or superficial engagement. The key lies in approaching these communities as powerful tools for growth while maintaining clear boundaries and intentional practice.

This expanded community framework provides unprecedented opportunities for mindset development, allowing participants to grow through exposure to diverse perspectives while maintaining focus on personal learning goals. When engaged thoughtfully, these communities become catalysts for sustained development and innovation.

The Integration of Digital and Human Intelligence

As we navigate the complexities of the digital age, the most effective approach to mindset development combines the best of both digital and human capabilities. This integration allows us to leverage technological advantages while maintaining the essential human elements of growth and development.

Research shows that combining human wisdom with AI capabilities produces better results than when either works alone. The most successful approaches emerge when we leverage technology's computational power while engaging distinctly human strengths, our ability to contextualize information, draw novel connections, and apply emotional intelligence to complex situations. This approach recognizes that technology works best, not as a replacement for human capabilities, but as a tool to enhance our natural cognitive and emotional processes.

The successful development of a healthy modern mindset requires understanding both the challenges and opportunities of our digital environment. By approaching technology with awareness and intention, we can create a relationship with digital tools that enhance rather than diminish our human capabilities.

Practical Applications: Mastering Your Mind in the Digital Age

The strategies that follow combine the best of what we know about brain science, with real-world testing. Each one targets a specific challenge of digital life while supporting and strengthening the others. For example, when you practice better attention control, you'll find it easier to set digital boundaries. When you set better boundaries, you'll find yourself more aware of how technology affects your energy and focus. These ten strategies were selected not just because they work individually, but because they work together to help you build a healthier relationship with technology.

1. Develop a Digital Consciousness Practice: Set three specific check-in times during your day to

assess your digital state. Notice your energy levels, emotional state, and mental clarity. Your early day assessment might reveal patterns about how different apps affect your startup routine, while evening check-ins can highlight which digital activities enhance or drain your mental resources.

2. Create Mindful Technology Boundaries: Establish clear limits around your digital device usage. Choose specific times for checking email and social media, designate tech free zones in your home, and set up automated 'do not disturb' periods. These boundaries aren't about restriction, but about creating space for your mind to process and integrate information effectively.

3. Practice Information Filtering: Develop a systematic approach to managing information input. Create three categories for incoming information, "need to know now," "might be useful later," and "interesting but not essential." This triage system helps your brain allocate attention more efficiently, reducing cognitive load while ensuring important information isn't missed.

4. Implement Attention Training: Choose one daily activity (like eating lunch or walking) and perform it without any digital devices, focusing completely on the experience. As your attention strengthens, you'll notice increased ability to focus during important digital tasks and easier transitions between online and offline activities.

5. Design Your Digital Environment: Systematically organize your digital spaces. Unfollow accounts that don't serve your growth, organize apps by purpose rather than habit, and create separate

profiles for different activities. Your digital environment shapes your thinking patterns just as much as your physical space does.

6. Exercise Social Media Mindfulness: Before each social media session, set a clear intention for what you want to accomplish. Use a timer for your sessions. Pay attention to how different types of content and interactions affect your mental state. This awareness helps transform social media from a passive habit into a tool for purposeful connection.

7. Establish Digital to Physical Balance: For every hour spent in digital activities, schedule a corresponding period of physical or analog activity. This rhythm helps your brain integrate information and maintain healthy neural patterns. The contrast between digital and physical engagement enhances both experiences.

8. Create Clear Digital Paths: Make your digital work smoother by thoughtfully organizing frequent tasks. When processing emails, creating documents, or managing files, look for ways to reduce jumping between tools. Group similar activities together, learn simple shortcuts, and arrange your workspace to maintain focus. When you find yourself frequently jumping between tools or getting stuck in digital tangles, pause to consider a simpler way through. This mindful organization helps your brain stay clear and energized.

9. Practice Digital Detachment: Start with short periods of complete digital disconnection. Begin with 30 minutes, then gradually increase to

several hours or a full day. Notice how your thought patterns and attention span shift during these periods. This practice builds confidence in your ability to function effectively offline.

10. Build Resilience Through Incremental Challenges: Gradually increase your tolerance for reduced digital stimulation. Start by turning off non-essential notifications, then progress to longer periods without checking devices. Each small success strengthens your capacity for focused attention and reduces digital dependency.

Begin with one or two strategies that feel most manageable and align with your current challenges. Implement them consistently for at least two weeks before adding more. Remember that developing a healthy relationship with technology is a gradual process, focus on progress rather than perfection, and adjust these practices to fit your specific needs and circumstances.

Remember, developing a healthy mindset in the digital age isn't about rejecting technology or trying to live without it. Instead, it's about learning to use digital tools mindfully and intentionally, while maintaining our fundamental human capacities for deep thought, emotional connection, and authentic growth. With conscious effort and the right strategies, we can harness the power of the digital age while protecting and enhancing our mental well-being.

Chapter 2: Mindfulness in the Modern World

As we navigate the complexities of modern life, the ancient practice of mindfulness has emerged as a powerful antidote to the stresses and distractions of our digital age. Now embraced by mainstream psychology, neuroscience, and organizations worldwide, mindfulness offers proven approaches for managing modern challenges while maintaining our essential humanity. Building on the neuroplasticity principles we explored in Chapter 1, mindfulness serves as a foundational tool for developing the mental capabilities needed to thrive in our rapidly evolving world.

The Evolution of Mindfulness

Mindfulness, at its core, is the practice of paying attention to the present moment with openness, curiosity, and non-judgment. While its roots can be traced back over 2,500 years to Buddhist practices, mindfulness gained broader adoption in the late 1970s through Jon Kabat-Zinn's Mindfulness-Based Stress Reduction (MBSR) program. This evolution represents a unique bridge between ancient wisdom and contemporary science, making mindfulness more accessible and applicable to modern challenges, while maintaining its essential transformative power.

Dr. Richard Davidson, founder of the Center for Healthy Minds at the University of Wisconsin-Madison, has conducted groundbreaking research on how mindfulness affects the brain. His studies using advanced neuroimaging techniques have demonstrated that regular mindfulness practice can actually reshape the brain's physical structure and function. This is particularly relevant in our digital age, as research from his lab shows that mindfulness training can strengthen areas of the brain associated with attention control and emotional regulation precisely the mental capabilities challenged by our technology saturated environment.

Neuroscience research has revealed how mindfulness creates measurable changes in our brains:

1. Prefrontal Cortex Enhancement: Our attention and decision-making command center becomes more robust through mindfulness practice. When notifications constantly compete for your attention during any focused activity, a strengthened prefrontal cortex lets you acknowledge these distractions without losing your concentration, maintaining your focus on what matters most.

2. Default Mode Network Regulation: The brain's rumination and worry center becomes less dominant with regular practice. Where you might once have spent sleepless nights replaying past conversations or worrying about future events, your mind naturally settles into restful quiet, leading to better sleep and clearer thinking.

3. Neural Pathway Development: Strengthened neural pathways create space between stimulus and response. Instead of reacting instantly to a frustrating message or comment, you can pause, process your emotional response, and respond thoughtfully in a way that maintains relationships and resolves issues.

4. Enhanced Neuroplasticity: The brain's ability to form new neural pathways becomes more

efficient, supporting adaptation and learning. Whether you're mastering a new skill, adapting to technology changes, or developing new habits, your enhanced neural flexibility helps you navigate changes with greater ease and confidence.

5. Amygdala Response Reduction: The brain's fear center becomes more regulated, building resilience to daily pressures. From handling everyday challenges to facing major life changes, a well-regulated amygdala helps you maintain composure and think clearly under pressure.

Mindfulness Practices for the Digital Age

Mindfulness extends far beyond meditation, offering diverse ways to cultivate present moment awareness in our daily lives. Contemporary practitioners find that mindful approaches enhance digital experiences, bringing conscious attention and intention to how we engage with technology.

Research from Dr. Nicholas Van Dam at the University of Melbourne's Contemplative Studies Centre shows how effectively mindfulness adapts to our digital reality. His studies reveal several key approaches to transforming our relationship with digital tools:

- Bringing intention to device use rather than operating from habit
- Developing conscious awareness in digital communications

- Creating purposeful transitions between online and offline activities
- Setting mindful boundaries around technology engagement

Those who develop these mindful technology habits demonstrate better attention control and report more satisfying digital interactions. Building on the neuroplasticity principles we explored earlier, this conscious engagement creates new patterns of interaction with technology. Rather than letting technology drive our behavior, mindful awareness helps us maintain intentionality in our digital experiences. This research suggests that conscious engagement, rather than digital escape, allows us to harness technology's benefits while maintaining mental well-being.

Mindful Moments

As demands on our time increase, integrating mindfulness into daily activities becomes essential. Research by Dr. Amishi Jha, director of contemplative neuroscience at the University of Miami, demonstrates that brief periods of mindful attention significantly strengthen our cognitive control. Her studies reveal how consistent mindful moments improve focus and stress management, vital skills for our fast-paced digital world.

Simple practices woven throughout the day can transform routine moments into opportunities for presence:

1. Digital Pauses: Before engaging with email or social media, take three conscious breaths while feeling your feet planted firmly on the ground. This intentional pause creates space for awareness

before encountering potentially stressful information.

2. Mindful Transitions: Between activities, pause briefly to notice your posture, breathing, and mental state. This conscious transition helps complete one experience before beginning another, reducing mental carryover and improving focus.

3. Environmental Awareness: Transform common signals like phone notifications, doorways, or traffic lights into reminders for presence. Each ping or threshold becomes an invitation to check in with your current experience, turning potential interruptions into moments of awareness.

4. Sensory Check-ins: During everyday activities like drinking water or washing hands, fully engage with physical sensations, the temperature, texture, and movement. These brief moments of complete sensory attention strengthen your natural capacity for presence.

5. Breathing Space: When feeling overwhelmed, take a 30 second breathing space, notice your current experience, gather attention to your breath, then expand awareness to your whole body. This quick reset helps maintain balance during challenging moments.

The effectiveness of these practices lies not in their duration but in their quality and consistency. Each mindful moment, however brief, interrupts automatic patterns and reinforces conscious presence. Over time, these small practices build a natural capacity for mindful engagement with all aspects of life.

Mindfulness in Daily Life and Work

The integration of mindfulness into daily life has become increasingly crucial as the boundaries between work, home, and digital spaces continue to blur. These evolving patterns present both challenges and opportunities for maintaining presence and awareness in our interconnected world.

Research from Dr. Ellen Langer, professor of psychology at Harvard University and pioneer in mindfulness research, demonstrates how conscious awareness transforms our daily experiences. Her studies show that bringing mindful attention to our activities, especially during transitions and role shifts, significantly improves both performance and well-being. People who develop consistent mindfulness practices demonstrate greater adaptability in navigating between work and personal responsibilities, particularly important in our increasingly fluid digital workspaces.

This mindful integration manifests in several key areas:

1. Boundary Management: Mindfulness helps establish clear transitions between different life domains. Rather than letting work seep into personal time or carrying home stress into work, mindful awareness enables us to recognize these boundaries and honor them. Simple practices like taking three conscious breaths before opening your work computer or closing your laptop with intention can create meaningful separations in an otherwise blended day.

2. Task Engagement: Conscious attention to our activities enhances both efficiency and

satisfaction. When responding to emails, mindful engagement helps maintain focus rather than falling into automatic reactions. During meetings, present moment awareness improves listening quality and contribution value. Even routine tasks become opportunities for presence rather than mere items to check off a list.

3. Stress Recognition: Mindfulness develops our ability to notice stress signals early, before they escalate. Physical tension, emotional reactions, and mental fatigue become clearer when viewed through the lens of conscious awareness. This early recognition allows for timely adjustments, whether taking a short break, adjusting priorities, or seeking support.

4. Relationship Navigation: In our connected world, relationships span multiple contexts, professional, personal, and digital. Mindful awareness helps maintain appropriate boundaries while fostering authentic connection. Whether managing team dynamics, family responsibilities, or online interactions, presence enables clearer communication and more meaningful engagement.

5. Energy Management: Rather than pushing through fatigue or ignoring natural rhythms, mindfulness helps us recognize and respect our energy patterns. This awareness enables better choices about when to engage in demanding tasks, when to take breaks, and how to structure our day for optimal balance and effectiveness.

This integration of mindfulness into daily life and work isn't about adding more tasks to our schedule. Instead, it's about bringing quality attention to what we're already doing. Through consistent practice, mindfulness becomes less of a separate activity and more of a natural way of engaging with all aspects of life, helping us maintain balance amid complexity and change.

Mindful Communication

Perhaps nowhere is the value of mindfulness more evident than in our communications, whether digital or face-to-face. Research by Dr. Daniel Siegel, clinical professor of psychiatry at UCLA and executive director of the Mindsight Institute, shows how mindful awareness fundamentally changes our capacity for connection. His studies on interpersonal neurobiology reveal that when we bring present moment attention to our interactions, we activate brain regions associated with empathy and emotional understanding, enhancing our ability to truly listen and communicate effectively.

Mindful awareness transforms both the quality and depth of our communications. During conversations, we can fully absorb what others are sharing, noticing tone, pace, and underlying emotions rather than planning our next response. Before important messages, particularly in digital exchanges where context can be lost, a mindful pause helps us check our intentions and emotional state. This awareness helps us recognize physical tension or emotional reactions in challenging discussions, allowing us to respond thoughtfully rather than reactively.

The benefits extend across all forms of interaction. In face-to-face settings, we become more attuned to facial expressions and body language, while in virtual environments, we can better sense engagement and connection through screens. Whether leading a team meeting, sharing family conversations, or navigating professional relationships, mindful awareness strengthens our capacity to understand others and communicate with genuine presence.

Creating Mindful Spaces

The importance of designated spaces for attention and presence has emerged as a key principle for modern life. Dr. Paul Gilbert, founder of Compassion Focused Therapy and researcher at the University of Derby, shows through his work on mental well-being how physical and mental boundaries help us shift between different modes of functioning. Creating deliberate boundaries supports our natural capacity for focused attention and presence.

This principle applies equally to physical and digital spaces. In the home, this might mean creating device free zones, a reading corner without digital distractions, or a dining area where conversation flows freely. In the workplace, whether remote or in office, it involves designing deliberate transitions between activities, a clear desk for focused work, specific times for digital communication, or regular breaks between virtual meetings. These thoughtful boundaries help distinguish between different modes of engagement, supporting both productivity and presence.

By consciously shaping our environment to support mindful awareness, we create external conditions that reinforce our internal practice. Whether working, connecting with others, or taking time for reflection, these intentional spaces help maintain the distinction between different activities while fostering deeper engagement in each moment.

Mindful Awareness in Leadership and Decision-Making

The application of mindfulness reveals its transformative potential most clearly when facing complex challenges. Research from Dr. Daniel Goleman, psychologist and author of *Emotional Intelligence*, and Dr. Richard Davidson, neuroscientist at the University of Wisconsin-Madison, demonstrates how mindfulness fundamentally alters our approach to challenges and decision-making.

Their collaborative research shows that sustained mindfulness practice enhances our capacity to remain clear and balanced in difficult situations, particularly valuable for leaders and decision-makers. Instead of falling into old habits or rushing to quick fixes, practitioners develop the ability to see situations more clearly and choose more effective responses. This enhanced awareness benefits everyone, from business leaders, to parents, to students.

Their research reveals how mindful awareness enhances key leadership capabilities:

1. Clearer Decision-Making: Moving from reactive choices to responsive decisions by creating space between stimulus and response. This allows us to evaluate situations more thoroughly and consider long-term implications before taking action.

2. Better Understanding of Emotions: Developing the capacity to recognize emotional patterns in ourselves and others, leading to more skillful

navigation of challenging interpersonal situations and improved emotional intelligence.

3. Bigger Picture Thinking: Cultivating the ability to step back from immediate challenges and recognize broader patterns and relationships, enabling more strategic and systemic approaches to complex situations.

4. Fresh Problem Solving: Developing mental flexibility that allows us to break free from habitual thinking patterns and explore innovative solutions, particularly valuable in rapidly changing environments.

5. Steady Presence: Building the capacity to maintain mental clarity and emotional balance under pressure, allowing for more consistent leadership and decision-making even in turbulent circumstances.

Research by Professor William George at Harvard Business School supports these findings across different situations. His studies of mindful leadership show that regular practitioners make better decisions under pressure and find more creative solutions to problems, both at work and in their personal lives.

The benefits of mindful leadership create ripple effects throughout organizations and families. When leaders develop greater mindful awareness, their enhanced presence creates environments where team members feel safer sharing ideas and taking creative risks. Similarly, when parents cultivate mindful awareness, they create spaces where family members feel truly heard and understood. The principle remains consistent, enhanced awareness leads to improved relationships and outcomes.

This ripple effect becomes especially valuable during times of change. Mindful awareness helps us notice when we're acting from fear or old habits, giving us the chance to pause and choose a better response. Whether you're adapting to new technology or handling changes in important relationships, the ability to respond thoughtfully rather than react automatically makes all the difference.

Mindfulness in the Age of AI

The relationship between mindfulness and artificial intelligence represents one of the most fascinating developments in modern practice. As AI becomes more integrated into our daily lives, mindfulness offers a way to maintain our human connection while benefiting from technological advances. Research from Dr. Adam Gazzaley, professor of neurology at UCSF and executive director of *Neuroscape*, reveals how technology and contemplative practice can work together to enhance human cognitive capabilities while preserving our essential awareness.

Gazzaley's work demonstrates that thoughtfully designed digital tools can enhance human attention and awareness. His research shows that the integration of technology with mindfulness practices creates powerful feedback loops for learning and development, while emphasizing the importance of maintaining human capacity. Like a musician who uses recording technology to enhance their practice while developing artistry through direct playing, mindfulness practitioners benefit most when technology supports, rather than substitutes for fundamental practice.

The key to effective integration lies in approaching technology as an enhancing tool that supports rather than replaces direct experience. When we bring mindful awareness to our interactions with technology, we can make more intentional choices about engagement, creating a balanced approach that strengthens, rather than diminishes our capacity for presence.

Practical Applications: Implementing Mindfulness in Modern Life

The strategies that follow bridge ancient mindfulness wisdom with modern day realities. Each practice has been carefully adapted to fit into the rhythm of contemporary life while preserving the essence of mindful awareness. These aren't separate techniques to master, but complementary practices that reinforce each other. When you create mindful transitions in your day, you naturally become more aware of your relationship with technology. As you develop awareness in your communications, you find yourself more present in your relationships. Together, these strategies create a practical framework for bringing mindfulness into every aspect of your daily experience.

1. Create Mindful Transitions: Design small mindfulness practices for transitions between activities, using the moments between tasks as natural pause points. When you finish a video call, take three conscious breaths before checking your next notification. As you switch from work to personal time, do a brief body scan. These micro-moments of awareness help your brain shift gears more effectively, reducing the mental residue that often carries over between activities.

2. Establish Digital Mindfulness Anchors: Choose specific digital actions as reminders for mindful awareness. Each time you enter your password, feel your fingers on the keyboard and take one conscious breath. When your phone buzzes, pause to notice your physical reaction before responding. These digital interruptions, typically sources of distraction, become opportunities for renewed presence.

3. Develop Awareness Triggers: Select specific locations and signals as mindfulness reminders. Your office doorway becomes a reminder to check your posture and energy. Your desk chair prompts awareness of tension patterns. Common sounds and spaces, like phone notifications or red lights, become invitations for presence. By linking awareness to your environment, you create a web of mindfulness reminders throughout your day.

4. Implement Mindful Communication Practices: Create conscious practices around all forms of communication. Before sending important messages, take a mindful pause to notice your intention and emotional state. During conversations, practice periodic awareness of your facial expressions and body language. These practices enhance both your presence and the clarity of your communication.

5. Design Mindful Work Intervals: Structure your time using your natural rhythms of energy and attention. Work focused for 25 minutes, then take a 5-minute mindfulness break. During these breaks, check your energy level while practicing simple awareness exercises, gentle stretching, conscious breathing, or mindful walking. This

rhythm honors your need for both focused work and recovery time.

6. Create Sensory Awareness Exercises: Develop regular practices that engage your senses fully. During meals, notice the temperature, texture, and subtle flavors of your food. While walking, feel the distinct sensations in your feet and legs. These practices strengthen your brain's ability to stay present with direct experience rather than getting lost in abstract thought.

7. Develop Body-Mind Integration: Practice conscious movement throughout your day. When sitting, notice your posture and make micro-adjustments. While walking, sync your breath with your steps. During moments of tension, scan for physical holding patterns and consciously release them. These practices strengthen the connection between physical awareness and mental states, deepening mindfulness through embodied experience.

8. Practice Stress and Emotional Awareness: Develop regular check-ins to monitor your stress levels and emotional state. Notice early warning signs like physical tension, racing thoughts, or emotional reactivity. When these signals arise, take a 30 second breathing space to reset. During interactions, pause to acknowledge emotions before they escalate. This awareness helps you recognize and respond to stress early, preventing overwhelm and building emotional resilience.

9. Cultivate Mindful Relationships: Create practices for bringing presence into your interactions. Before important conversations, take a moment to

ground yourself. During discussions, notice when your mind starts planning responses rather than truly listening. These practices enhance both the quality of your relationships and your ability to remain present with others.

10. Foster Leadership Presence: Develop practices that enhance your presence and effectiveness in any leadership role, whether at work or home. Before making important decisions, pause to check your mental state and potential biases. During group interactions, maintain awareness of the overall dynamic. These practices improve your clarity and effectiveness in guiding others.

Begin with one or two practices that resonate most naturally with your daily routines. Consistency with a simple practice builds stronger neural pathways than sporadic attempts at multiple techniques. Remember that mindfulness is not about achieving a particular state, but about developing the capacity to be present with whatever is arising. Let your practice grow with your changing needs while maintaining steady connection with these core practices.

Remember, mindfulness in the modern world isn't about escaping our digital reality or returning to a simpler past. Instead, it's about finding ways to bring present moment awareness and intentional living into our contemporary lives. By adapting ancient practices to modern contexts while maintaining their essential principles, we can develop a more balanced and aware way of living in our technologically enhanced world. These mindfulness practices provide practical tools for navigating our complex modern lives. The key lies not in perfecting every technique, but in consistently returning to present moment awareness, one conscious breath at a time.

Chapter 3: Cultivating Resilience and Adaptability in Uncertain Times

In our rapidly evolving world, the ability to bounce back from setbacks and adapt to new circumstances has become a fundamental skill for thriving in modern life. Building on the mindfulness practices we explored, resilience and adaptability represent the next crucial steps in developing a mind capable of navigating uncertainty with confidence. Whether facing technological disruptions, personal challenges, or professional changes, these capabilities help us not just survive, but grow through difficult times.

The Science of Resilience

Recent research has transformed our understanding of resilience. What scientists once viewed as a fixed personality trait, we now recognize as a set of skills that anyone can develop and strengthen. This shift in perspective opens exciting possibilities for personal growth and development in both our professional and personal lives.

Dr. George Bonanno, professor of clinical psychology at Columbia University and director of the Loss, Trauma, and Emotion Lab, has conducted groundbreaking research on human resilience. His studies demonstrate that resilience isn't about being tough or stoic, but rather about maintaining flexibility in our responses to life's challenges. Through decades of research, he has shown that resilience is both more common than previously thought and more teachable than we once believed.

Research published in *Nature Neuroscience* by Dr. Elizabeth Phelps, and colleagues at Harvard University, reveals the neural basis of emotional resilience. Using advanced brain imaging, they demonstrated that individuals who show greater resilience have stronger connections between their prefrontal cortex (involved in planning and decision-making) and amygdala (involved in emotion processing). This improved neural connectivity allows for better emotion regulation during stressful situations, suggesting that we can actually strengthen these brain networks through targeted practice.

The Mind-Body Connection in Resilience

Understanding resilience requires acknowledging the profound connection between mental and physical responses to challenges. Dr. Bruce McEwen's pioneering research at Rockefeller University revolutionized our understanding of this connection. His work demonstrates that resilience isn't just a mental state, but a whole-body experience involving complex interactions between our brain, hormones, and nervous system. When we understand how challenges affect both mind and body, we can develop more comprehensive strategies for building resilience.

Research in neurobiology and stress response has identified several key factors that build resilience:

1. Supportive Connections: The power of relationships in fostering resilience. McEwen's

research shows that positive social relationships actively regulate our stress response system. For example, when facing a challenging work project, discussing it with a trusted mentor not only provides practical guidance but also triggers biological responses that help us think more clearly and feel more capable.

2. Meaningful Engagement: Finding purpose in challenges helps maintain motivation and direction. When confronted with a career setback, reframing it as an opportunity to develop new skills transforms the experience from purely stressful to potentially valuable. This shift in perspective changes both our psychological and physiological responses to the situation.

3. Physical Restoration: The body's role in bouncing back from stress. Studies show that practices like deep breathing or mindful walking don't just make us feel better, they actively reset our nervous system. Even a brief walk during a stressful day can restore our capacity to think clearly and respond effectively.

4. Cognitive Flexibility: The ability to view situations from multiple perspectives. When a team project faces obstacles, those who can consider different approaches and remain flexible show better stress recovery. This mental flexibility directly influences our body's ability to maintain balance under pressure.

5. Development Mindset: Understanding that challenges build capacity. Each difficulty we navigate strengthens our ability to handle future obstacles. Like building physical strength through

exercise, we can build psychological resilience through gradually taking on and learning from challenges.

McEwen's research on allostasis, how our bodies maintain stability through change, demonstrates why these factors work together so effectively. His studies show that resilience develops through the coordinated effort of both psychological and biological systems, making a strong case for approaches that address both mind and body in building lasting psychological strength.

Building Micro-Resilience in Daily Life

While major challenges test our resilience, it's the small recoveries throughout our day that build this capability over time. Research on stress adaptation shows that these minor recoveries work much like physical training, each small "workout" strengthens our capacity to handle larger challenges. Just as we developed mindful moments in our earlier practice, we can create "resilience moments", brief opportunities to practice bouncing back from minor setbacks.

These micro-resilience practices work in several key ways:

1. Stress Recovery: Quick reset practices that help us bounce back from minor frustrations throughout the day. A few deep breaths after a challenging email or a moment of mindful awareness during a busy commute can prevent stress accumulation.

2. Energy Management: Strategic breaks that maintain our resilience capacity. Alternating

focused work with brief recovery periods helps sustain our ability to handle challenges.

3. Emotional Regulation: Small opportunities to practice managing reactions. When a meeting runs late or plans change unexpectedly, these moments become chances to practice flexible responses.

4. Pattern Recognition: Becoming aware of our typical stress responses in low stakes situations. This awareness helps us respond more effectively when bigger challenges arise.

5. Confidence Building: Accumulating evidence of our ability to handle difficulties. Each successful navigation of a small challenge builds trust in our resilience capacity.

The key lies in treating these challenges not as interruptions to our preferred routine, but as opportunities to strengthen our resilience capacity. Like building any skill, it's consistent practice in everyday moments that develops lasting strength.

Adaptability in a Rapidly Changing World

While resilience helps us bounce back from setbacks, adaptability enables us to thrive amid constant change. Research from Harvard Business School's organizational behavior division shows that in today's environment, adaptability isn't just about surviving change, it's about maintaining effectiveness and finding opportunities in new situations. Their studies of successful leaders and organizations demonstrate that adaptation has become a fundamental skill for thriving in our fast-paced world.

Research shows that highly adaptable individuals share several key capabilities:

1. Cognitive Flexibility: The ability to adjust thinking patterns as circumstances change. Rather than rigidly adhering to one approach, adaptable people readily consider alternatives.

2. Emotional Agility: Skill in managing emotional responses to change. This involves acknowledging feelings about changes while maintaining the ability to move forward constructively.

3. Learning Orientation: A natural curiosity about new situations and willingness to experiment. Instead of seeing changes as threats, adaptable individuals view them as learning opportunities.

4. Comfort with Uncertainty: The capacity to function effectively even when outcomes are unclear. This comfort with ambiguity allows for better decision-making in complex situations.

5. Strategic Optimism: The ability to maintain a constructive outlook while acknowledging challenges realistically. This balanced perspective supports both resilience and continued adaptation.

These capabilities don't develop in isolation, but rather strengthen and support each other through practice. As we become more cognitively flexible, we naturally develop greater comfort with uncertainty. As our emotional agility increases, we find it easier to maintain strategic optimism. Together, these adaptive skills enable us not just to endure change, but to actively engage with it in ways that promote growth and development.

The Digital Dimension

Modern resilience and adaptability require specific strategies for managing technology related challenges. Building on our digital mindfulness practices, we can develop what researchers call "digital resilience", the ability to bounce back from and adapt to technological stresses and changes.

Studies from the Oxford Internet Institute demonstrate how our relationship with technology significantly impacts our overall resilience. Their research reveals several key approaches that help build digital resilience:

1. Digital Boundaries: Creating clear containers for technology use that prevent constant drain on our resources. This might mean designating specific times for email or social media, establishing tech free zones, or setting clear limits on notification interruptions.

2. Recovery Rituals: Establishing practices that help us bounce back from digital intensity. A brief walk after video calls or stretching between screen sessions can reset our system. These aren't just breaks, they're strategic recovery points that maintain our cognitive resilience.

3. Adaptation Strategies: Developing flexible approaches to new technologies. Rather than resisting or rushing into every new tool, we can thoughtfully evaluate and integrate helpful

innovations while maintaining our essential work patterns.

4. Connection Balance: Maintaining a healthy mix of digital and in person interactions. Strong relationships support resilience across both domains, and conscious attention to this balance prevents digital overwhelm while preserving meaningful connections.

5. Technical Growth: Viewing technological challenges as opportunities to build both competence and confidence. Each new tool mastered strengthens our adaptability muscle, making future adaptations easier and more natural.

These strategies work together to create a sustainable approach to technology use that builds resilience rather than depleting it. By implementing them thoughtfully, we can harness technology's benefits while protecting our capacity for resilience and growth.

Collective Resilience

While resilience starts with individual capacity, it flourishes in supportive environments. Research demonstrates that our ability to navigate challenges significantly increases when we're part of resilient networks and communities. This isn't just about having support during difficult times, it's about creating environments where both individual and collective resilience can grow stronger together.

The power of collective resilience becomes evident in how groups respond to shared challenges. When faced with difficulties, resilient teams and communities draw upon their combined strengths, sharing not just resources but also knowledge and emotional support. This mutual reinforcement creates a multiplier effect, where individual and group resilience build upon each other. Research from organizational psychology shows that teams who develop this collective strength can navigate complex challenges more effectively than even highly resilient individuals working alone.

This collective dimension of resilience operates through several key mechanisms. Groups that effectively pool their resources and share knowledge develop greater adaptive capacity than their individual members might possess separately. When teams maintain strong communication and support structures, they create environments where members feel safe taking calculated risks and exploring innovative solutions. Perhaps most importantly, collective resilience provides a buffer against exhaustion and overwhelm, when one member needs to step back and recharge, others can step forward to maintain momentum.

The benefits extend beyond immediate challenge response. Groups with strong collective resilience consistently demonstrate better problem-solving capabilities, increased innovation, and improved long-term outcomes. They show enhanced ability to learn from experience and adapt their approaches over time. This creates an ongoing cycle of development where supporting others ultimately strengthens everyone, building both individual and collective capacity for facing future challenges.

Future Focused Resilience

As we look toward an increasingly complex future, new dimensions of resilience and adaptability continue to emerge. Research from MIT's Initiative on the Digital Economy shows that tomorrow's challenges will require us to develop greater psychological flexibility while maintaining deep human connections. Their studies emphasize that success lies not in predicting specific challenges, but in building capabilities that help us navigate uncertainty while staying grounded in our fundamental humanity.

Technology plays a particularly nuanced role in this future focused resilience. While artificial intelligence and other emerging technologies offer powerful tools for supporting human adaptation, they also create new challenges that require fresh approaches to resilience. The goal isn't to become more machine like in our responses to stress, but rather to enhance uniquely human capabilities for creative adaptation and emotional recovery.

This enhancement of human capabilities takes various forms. Anticipatory resilience, the ability to prepare for potential challenges while remaining flexible enough to handle unexpected developments, represents one crucial development. Unlike rigid planning, which can break under pressure, anticipatory resilience involves maintaining a dynamic readiness for change. It's about developing the mental and emotional agility to pivot effectively when circumstances shift.

Research from Harvard's Human Technology Interaction Group demonstrates that successful adaptation requires a balanced approach. Their studies show that resilience in the digital age isn't about having the most advanced technology or the most detailed contingency plans.

Instead, it emerges from maintaining human connection and creativity while thoughtfully integrating new tools and approaches.

This insight has profound implications for how we prepare for future challenges. Rather than trying to predict and plan for every possible scenario, we can focus on building core capabilities that serve us across various situations:

1. Learning Agility: Developing the ability to quickly acquire and apply new knowledge, whether facing technological changes or shifts in our personal lives. This involves not just mastering new skills but understanding how to learn effectively in rapidly changing environments. It means recognizing which knowledge is fundamental and which needs regular updating.

2. Cultural Intelligence: Building the capacity to navigate increasingly diverse and interconnected social environments with empathy and understanding. This extends beyond basic awareness to include active engagement with different perspectives and approaches. In our globally connected world, this capability becomes essential for both personal and professional resilience.

3. Environmental Awareness: Cultivating sensitivity to changes in our surroundings, and flexibility in our responses to environmental challenges. This includes recognizing early signals of change, understanding systemic connections, and developing adaptive responses that work within larger contexts. This awareness helps us

anticipate and respond to shifts before they become crises.

The future of resilience also involves rethinking traditional approaches to stress and recovery. New research in psychophysiology reveals that resilience isn't just about "pushing through" challenges, it's about learning to flow with change while maintaining our center. This might mean taking micro-recovery breaks throughout the day, practicing regular skill updates, or engaging in ongoing scenario exploration to maintain adaptability.

Practical Applications: Building Resilience and Adaptability

The strategies that follow provide a comprehensive framework for developing resilience and adaptability in modern life. These practices build upon each other, creating a robust foundation for navigating uncertainty while continuing to grow and thrive. While some approaches might resonate more strongly than others, each contributes to building a more resilient and adaptable mind.

1. Develop Stress Inoculation Routines: Start with small, manageable challenges and gradually increase difficulty. When public speaking creates anxiety, begin by sharing one insight in a small group setting, then progress to leading short segments, and eventually to presenting full proposals. Each successful navigation of discomfort recalibrates your stress response system and builds confidence in your ability to handle larger challenges.

2. Create Learning Experiments: Design small tests for trying new approaches to familiar tasks. Choose one routine activity each week and deliberately alter your method. You might take a different route home, try a new problem-solving approach, or engage with people outside your usual circle. Document what you notice about your reactions, resistance, and discoveries. These controlled experiments build your capacity for flexibility while maintaining a sense of security.

3. Build Recovery Rituals: Establish specific practices for responding to immediate setbacks. Create a three-step reset routine, first acknowledge the challenge without judgment, then identify one piece of learning or insight, finally take one small action toward your goals. Practice this sequence with minor setbacks to build the neural pathways for resilience during larger challenges.

4. Cultivate Support Networks: Actively develop different types of support relationships. Connect with mentors for guidance, peers for skill sharing, and friends for emotional support. Schedule regular check-ins with these individuals, approaching each connection with clarity about your needs and what you can offer in return. This network becomes your resilience ecosystem.

5. Practice Perspective Shifting: Regularly examine situations from multiple viewpoints. When facing a challenge, intentionally view it through different lenses, as a learning opportunity, as a test of creativity, or as a chance to help others. Note how each view changes your response to the challenge, opening up new possibilities for action,

and building your capacity to adapt under pressure.

6. Design Adaptability Challenges: Create deliberate opportunities to experience new situations. Start with small changes that introduce unfamiliar elements, try new environments, explore different topics, or experiment with new ways of working. Gradually increase these explorations as your comfort grows. These experiences build confidence in handling unexpected changes.

7. Establish Reflection Practices: Create regular time for understanding patterns in your experiences. Keep a resilience journal documenting challenges faced, strategies used, and insights gained. Review this journal periodically to identify what consistently helps you bounce back. This reflection transforms experiences into wisdom that serves future challenges.

8. Develop Future Sensing: Create regular practices for staying attuned to emerging changes in your environment. Set aside time each week to explore new developments in your field, discuss future trends with colleagues, or examine how current changes might affect your path forward. This builds your anticipatory resilience while maintaining practical grounding in the present.

9. Connect and Apply Learning: Create regular opportunities for incorporating new learning and experiences into your existing frameworks. After trying new approaches or facing challenges, take time to connect these experiences with your established skills and knowledge. Regular review

sessions help you bridge new insights with proven practices, building adaptability while maintaining stability.

10. Build Sustainability Practices: Develop specific routines that help maintain your resilience capacity over time. Balance periods of challenge with dedicated recovery time, create clear boundaries between different life domains, and regularly assess your energy management. These practices ensure your resilience resources remain renewable rather than depleting over time.

Begin with practices that align naturally with your current situation. Focus on consistency rather than intensity, small, regular steps build more sustainable resilience than sporadic large efforts. Pay attention to how different practices affect your stress response and ability to handle change. Adjust these strategies to fit your specific circumstances, understanding that building resilience and adaptability is a highly personal journey.

Remember that developing these capabilities is an ongoing process, not a destination. Each challenge you face becomes an opportunity to strengthen your resilience and expand your adaptability. The key lies not in avoiding difficulty, but in approaching it with curiosity and openness to growth. As you continue to practice these strategies, you'll find yourself better equipped to navigate uncertainty while maintaining your sense of purpose and well-being.

Chapter 4: Harnessing Creativity and Imagination for Personal Growth

In an era where artificial intelligence increasingly handles routine tasks, our uniquely human qualities of creativity and imagination have become more valuable than ever. These aren't just special talents reserved for artists or inventors – they're essential capabilities we all possess and can develop to enhance every aspect of our lives. Building on the mindfulness and resilience we've explored in previous chapters, understanding and cultivating our creative potential becomes the next crucial step in developing a mind equipped for modern challenges.

The Science of Creative Thinking

Recent advances in neuroscience have transformed our understanding of creativity, revealing it as a complex interplay of various brain networks that we can actively strengthen. Research from Dr. Rex Jung at the University of New Mexico and colleagues has shown that creativity emerges from the dynamic interaction between different neural systems, rather than being localized to a single area of the brain.

Their neuroimaging studies demonstrate that creative thinking emerges from the coordinated activity of three key neural networks, each playing a distinct role in the creative process. Like a symphony orchestra where different sections work together to create music, these brain networks collaborate to produce creative insights and innovations.

Research demonstrates three key neural networks involved in creative thinking:

1. The Default Mode Network: This network is most active during periods of rest or mind-wandering and is associated with self-referential thinking, memory consolidation, and envisioning future scenarios. It facilitates the generation of novel ideas by allowing the brain to retrieve and recombine stored knowledge in new ways, helping integrate unrelated concepts, a process essential for creativity.

2. The Salience Network: This network plays a critical role in identifying and prioritizing stimuli or thoughts that are most relevant to current goals or emotional states. It acts as a mediator between the Default Mode and Executive Control Networks, ensuring that valuable ideas emerging from spontaneous thought are brought to conscious attention. Studies using functional MRI have demonstrated its activation when individuals assess the novelty or importance of creative ideas.

3. The Executive Control Network: This network is responsible for cognitive control and decision-making, particularly in tasks requiring focus, problem-solving, and goal-directed behavior. It regulates the refinement and implementation of creative ideas, ensuring they align with practical constraints and objectives. Research highlights its involvement in suppressing irrelevant information and maintaining attention on tasks, which is

essential for turning abstract ideas into actionable outcomes.

This understanding has profound implications for personal development. Just as we can strengthen our muscles through exercise, we can enhance our creative capabilities through specific practices that engage these neural networks. When someone says, "I'm just not creative," they're expressing a mindset, not a biological reality. Our brains are designed for creativity – we just need to learn how to access and develop this natural capacity.

Imagination in Problem Solving

While creativity often evokes images of art studios or innovation labs, imagination serves as a fundamental tool for solving everyday challenges. Research from Dr. Marvin Minsky at MIT's Media Lab demonstrates how mental simulation capabilities form the foundation of human problem solving. His work shows that our ability to imagine and mentally test scenarios before taking action gives us a unique advantage in navigating both daily challenges and complex problems.

Studies in cognitive psychology have mapped distinct aspects of imagination that contribute to sophisticated problem solving. These core capabilities work together as a coordinated system:

1. Mental Simulation: The ability to visualize and "test-run" different scenarios in our minds before taking action. This goes beyond simple visualization, it involves engaging multiple

sensory and emotional systems to create detailed mental models. Whether rehearsing a challenging conversation or planning a complex project, this capability allows us to refine our approach before committing to action.

2. Pattern Recognition: The capacity to identify meaningful connections between seemingly unrelated experiences and domains. This involves both recognizing existing patterns and creating novel connections. For example, understanding how ecosystem principles might inform organizational dynamics, or how musical rhythm concepts could improve project management.

3. Perspective Shifting: The ability to mentally adopt different viewpoints and frameworks for understanding situations. This involves not just seeing things from another angle, but temporarily inhabiting different ways of thinking. Such flexibility allows us to understand complex interpersonal dynamics and find innovative solutions to persistent problems.

4. Future Forecasting: The capability to construct and evaluate multiple possible futures, considering both likely outcomes and unexpected possibilities. This goes beyond simple prediction to include developing adaptive strategies for different scenarios. It enables both short-term planning and long-term strategic thinking.

Research from Stanford's Center for Design Research reveals how these imaginative capabilities form an integrated problem-solving system. When people actively engage all four aspects of imagination, they consistently develop more innovative and effective solutions. Like a master chef combining different techniques to create exceptional dishes, our minds blend these imaginative capabilities to transform challenges into opportunities for growth and innovation.

Creativity in the Digital Age

As artificial intelligence becomes more sophisticated, understanding the unique qualities of human creativity grows increasingly important. Research from Dr. Margaret Boden, a pioneer in the study of artificial intelligence and human creativity at the University of Sussex, demonstrates fundamental differences between computational and human creative processes. While AI excels at analyzing patterns and generating variations, human creativity uniquely enables us to make meaningful, emotionally resonant connections that transcend pure logic.

This human element of creativity manifests in various ways throughout our lives. A parent creating a bedtime story that perfectly addresses their child's current fears demonstrates creativity just as much as an entrepreneur developing a new business model. A home cook experimenting with flavors based on childhood memories exercises the same creative muscles as a scientist formulating a new hypothesis.

The relationship between human creativity and AI is evolving into an interesting partnership. Studies from MIT's Media Lab on human-AI collaboration reveal how these different types of intelligence can complement each other. Rather than replacing human creativity, AI often serves to enhance it. For instance, while AI can generate countless variations of a design, human creative judgment recognizes which version will resonate most deeply with people. While AI can analyze vast amounts of data, human imagination discovers meaningful patterns and implications that lead to innovative breakthroughs. This synergy suggests that the future of creativity lies not in competition between humans and machines, but in their thoughtful integration.

The Depth of Human Imagination

While artificial intelligence can process information at remarkable speeds, human imagination possesses unique qualities that set it apart. Research from Dr. Antonio Damasio, director of USC's Brain and Creativity Institute, reveals how emotions and personal experience fundamentally shape human creativity. His studies demonstrate that our imagination isn't just about generating new ideas, it's intimately connected with our emotions, memories, and sense of meaning. Each creative act draws upon our entire life experience, integrating rational thought with emotional understanding.

Personal experience profoundly influences how we imagine and create solutions. Our unique life experiences shape, not just what we create, but how we approach the creative process itself. This explains why different people, when presented with the same challenge, often envision entirely different possibilities and solutions.

We see this emotional-imaginative connection expressed throughout daily life. When a teacher develops a new way to explain a difficult concept, they're drawing not just on their knowledge of the subject, but on their understanding of their students' emotional and intellectual needs. When someone redecorates their living space, they're expressing not just aesthetic preferences but deeper feelings about comfort, security, and personal identity.

Nurturing Creative Development

Understanding creativity as a natural human capacity raises an important question, how can we best nurture and develop this essential capability? Research from Dr. Teresa Amabile, Professor of Business Administration at Harvard Business School and pioneer in creativity research, demonstrates that creative development flourishes under specific conditions. Her studies show that growth occurs most effectively at the intersection of challenge and safety, where we're stretched beyond our comfort zone while feeling secure enough to take creative risks.

Recent research has identified several key conditions that support creative development:

1. Psychological Safety: The confidence to explore new ideas without fear of judgment or ridicule. This involves creating environments where experimentation is encouraged, and mistakes are viewed as learning opportunities. Research shows that teams and individuals who feel psychologically safe generate more innovative solutions and take more creative risks.

2. Structured Freedom: Clear boundaries that provide direction while allowing room for exploration. This balance between constraints and flexibility creates a framework for creativity, like an artist working within the limitations of their medium while exploring infinite possibilities within

those boundaries. Studies indicate that some constraints actually enhance creativity by providing focus and direction.

3. Reflective Space: Regular opportunities to step back and process experiences. Dedicated time for reflection allows us to integrate new insights and recognize emerging patterns. Research shows that periods of conscious reflection significantly enhance creative problem-solving abilities.

4. Collaborative Support: Access to others who can offer feedback and inspiration while respecting individual creative processes. This involves both giving and receiving constructive input in ways that enhance rather than inhibit creative development. Studies demonstrate that diverse perspectives and supportive feedback accelerate creative growth.

Dr. Amabile's research emphasizes that these conditions apply universally across different domains of creativity. Whether in professional innovation, artistic expression, or everyday problem solving, these fundamental elements create an environment where creativity can flourish.

Ethics and Responsibility in Creative Work

As our creative capabilities become enhanced by technology, questions of ethics and responsibility take on new importance. Research from MIT's Media Ethics Initiative demonstrates that increased creative power, whether through AI, new technologies, or innovative approaches, brings with it greater responsibility to consider the broader impacts of our innovations. Their studies show that ethical considerations need to be integrated into the creative process from the beginning, not added as an afterthought.

This ethical dimension of creativity extends far beyond professional contexts. A parent choosing how to use AI-powered educational tools with their children engages with similar ethical considerations as a designer developing new technology. A community volunteer reimagining a local recycling program wrestles with the same questions of impact and unintended consequences as a corporate innovator. Dr. Luciano Floridi's work at Oxford's Digital Ethics Lab reveals how these ethical considerations appear at every scale of creative innovation, from personal choices to global initiatives.

The challenge lies in balancing creative freedom with responsible innovation. When we recognize that our creative choices can have far reaching effects, we must develop frameworks for evaluating potential impacts while maintaining the spontaneity and exploration essential to the creative process.

The Future of Human Creativity

As we look ahead, significant developments in neuroscience and technology are transforming our understanding of creative potential. Dr. David Eagleman's research at Stanford University demonstrates how the integration of neuroscience with emerging technologies is revealing new dimensions of human creativity. His work shows that as we better understand the brain's creative processes, we can develop more effective ways to enhance and express our natural creative abilities.

Virtual reality and augmented reality technologies are creating unprecedented opportunities for creative exploration. Stanford's Virtual Human Interaction Lab has shown how immersive environments enable us to experiment with ideas in ways previously impossible. Rather than simply imagining different possibilities, we can now experience them directly, walking through architectural designs before construction begins, testing educational approaches in simulated classrooms, or prototyping new concepts in virtual spaces. These tools amplify our creative capabilities by providing new environments for our imagination to explore.

The landscape of collaborative creativity is also evolving dramatically. Research from MIT's Center for Collective Intelligence reveals how digital platforms are revolutionizing creative collaboration. These technologies enable diverse groups to engage in creative problem-solving across geographical and cultural boundaries, combining perspectives in ways that weren't previously possible. Their studies show that the most successful creative collaborations emerge when technology facilitates, rather than directs, human creative exchange.

This evolution in creative tools and understanding holds profound implications for personal development. As automation increasingly handles routine tasks, our uniquely human capacity for creative thinking becomes more vital. However, this shift isn't about turning everyone into traditional artists or inventors. Instead, it's about recognizing and developing the creative intelligence we use every day, whether solving complex problems, building meaningful relationships, or navigating life's challenges. The future of creativity lies not in replacing human imagination with technology, but in finding new ways to amplify and express our innate creative potential.

Practical Applications: Developing Creativity and Imagination

The following strategies are designed to develop your creative capabilities in ways that serve both everyday challenges and larger aspirations. Each practice builds upon the mindfulness and resilience skills we've explored in previous chapters while preparing you for the more complex problem-solving we'll address later.

1. Design Pattern Integration Exercises: Create connections between different domains of your experience by identifying principles that transfer across areas of your life. Choose two different activities or areas you're familiar with and list their key elements. Look for unexpected parallels and potential applications. For example, consider how you organize your home and how you manage your work tasks what successful approaches from one area might help in the other?

2. Create Imagination Spaces: Designate both physical and digital environments that support creative thinking. Your physical space might be as simple as a comfortable chair with a notebook or as elaborate as a project wall for visual mapping. In the digital realm, create distraction free zones for focused creative work. When you enter these spaces, they signal your brain to shift into exploratory mode.

3. Integrate Creative Viewpoints: Combine different ways of seeing with emotional insight. Approach challenges through varied lenses, analytical, artistic, or practical. Notice how each viewpoint not only brings new ideas but stirs different emotions and insights. When you combine these varied perspectives with their emotional imprints, richer and more innovative solutions naturally emerge.

4. Implement Creative Constraints: Transform limitations into catalysts for innovation. Whether working with tight budgets, limited time, or specific requirements, use these boundaries to focus your creative energy. Research shows that appropriate constraints often spark more innovative thinking than unlimited options.

5. Develop Visual-Emotional Mapping: Create visual representations that capture both the logical and emotional aspects of concepts or challenges. Combine simple drawings, diagrams, or symbols with notes about associated feelings and intuitions. This practice integrates different modes of understanding, leading to richer insights.

6. Build Creative Rituals: Establish practices that prepare both mind and body for creative thinking. This might include arranging your space, playing specific music, or taking a mindful walk. Pay attention to which rituals help you feel both energized and centered, creating reliable pathways into creative states.

7. Explore Collaborative Creativity: Engage with both in person and digital platforms for creative exchange. Participate in brainstorming sessions,

online innovation communities, or creative partnerships. Focus on how different perspectives and approaches can combine to generate new possibilities while maintaining your unique creative voice.

8. Practice Solution Archaeology: Study inspiring solutions across different fields, examining both their technical development and emotional impact. Whether analyzing a well-designed product or a successful social initiative, understand not just how it works but why it resonates with people.

9. Create Insight Integration Systems: Develop methods for capturing and connecting creative insights throughout your day. Use a combination of digital tools and traditional notebooks, focusing on recording not just ideas but also the contexts and feelings that sparked them. Regularly reviewing these notes can uncover surprising patterns, connections, and new possibilities.

10. Design Future Scenario Explorations: Use both analytical thinking and emotional intelligence to imagine potential futures. Consider not just what might happen, but how different scenarios would feel and what opportunities they might present. This practice develops your capacity to envision and shape future possibilities rather than simply responding to them.

Begin with practices that naturally align with your current creative process and gradually incorporate others. Remember that developing creativity is not about forcing inspiration but about creating conditions where innovation can flourish naturally. Pay attention to which combinations of practices work best for you and adapt them to suit your unique creative style and needs.

As you experiment with these practices, notice which times of day and environmental conditions enhance your creative thinking. Some people find their imagination flows more freely in the early part of the day, others in the evening. Some think best while moving, others while sitting still. Trust your experience while remaining open to new possibilities.

Remember that creativity isn't a mystical quality possessed by a gifted few. It's a fundamental human capacity that we can all develop through practice and patience. In our rapidly changing world, the ability to think creatively, imagine new possibilities, and approach problems from fresh angles becomes increasingly valuable, not just in specific creative pursuits, but in every aspect of life.

Chapter 5: Unlocking the Power of the Subconscious Mind

As we've explored how to build mindfulness, resilience, and creativity, we've worked primarily with our conscious mind. Yet beneath these conscious efforts lies a powerful force that shapes much of our daily experience. the subconscious mind. Understanding and working with this deeper aspect of ourselves opens new possibilities for personal growth and transformation.

Think of your mind like a vast ocean. Your conscious thoughts represent the surface waves, visible, active, and easily noticed. But beneath these waves lies a deep, powerful current, your subconscious mind, that influences everything from your habits and reactions to your decisions and relationships. Just as we've learned to work with our conscious thoughts through mindfulness and creative practice, we can develop ways to understand and work with these deeper currents of our mind.

The Science of the Subconscious

Recent advances in neuroscience have transformed our understanding of how the subconscious mind works. Research from Dr. John Bargh at Yale University's Automaticity in Cognition, Motivation, and Evaluation Lab demonstrates how mental processes operating below our awareness profoundly influence our daily lives. His studies reveal that the subconscious mind isn't a single entity but rather a complex network of interconnected systems that shape our behaviors, emotions, and decisions.

Through extensive research combining brain imaging and behavioral studies, neuroscientists have identified several key networks that form our subconscious mental processes:

1. Implicit Learning Network: This network is responsible for automatically acquiring and executing skills through repeated practice. Think about when you first learned to drive: every action required conscious effort. Now, you can navigate complex traffic situations while holding a conversation because this network has automated those well-practiced skills. By understanding this process, we can approach new learning more effectively, knowing that with consistent effort, conscious actions will eventually transform into seamless, automatic performance.

2. Emotional Processing Network: Acting as our intuitive emotional radar, this network rapidly processes emotional information and guides our actions before we are consciously aware of why. For example, you might instinctively pull back from a situation that feels unsafe or lean toward someone who inspires trust and connection. Drawing on a lifetime of emotional experiences, it shapes our gut reactions and helps us navigate social and interpersonal dynamics with speed and precision. By understanding this network, we can enhance emotional intelligence and refine how we interpret and respond to emotional cues in ourselves and others.

3. Predictive Processing Network: Serving as our pattern recognition system, this network constantly compares current experiences with stored memories to anticipate what might happen next. For instance, you can sense when a familiar routine feels "off" or find your way in a new city by recognizing patterns that resemble places you know. This network helps us prepare for likely scenarios while staying adaptable to unexpected changes.

These networks work together seamlessly to support your daily life. For instance, when driving home from work, the Implicit Learning Network manages the mechanics of driving, freeing you from needing to consciously think about every action. Meanwhile, the Emotional Processing Network scans for potential dangers, such as a sudden change in traffic behavior, while the Predictive Processing Network anticipates patterns like congestion ahead or familiar turns on your route. Together, they operate in the background, allowing your conscious mind to focus on planning dinner, reflecting on your day, or simply enjoying the ride.

The Subconscious in Daily Life

Understanding how the subconscious mind influences our daily experiences can be transformative. Dr. Benjamin Libet's pioneering research at the University of California, San Francisco demonstrated how our subconscious shapes decision-making processes. His groundbreaking studies showed that neural activity associated with decisions begins several hundred milliseconds before we become consciously aware of our choices.

This understanding has been further advanced by more recent research at the Max Planck Institute for Human Cognitive and Brain Sciences. Using advanced brain imaging techniques, researchers found that patterns of brain activity can indicate a person's decisions several seconds before they become consciously aware of having made a choice. Whether selecting lunch options or preparing for important conversations, our subconscious processes are actively shaping our responses before conscious awareness engages.

However, this doesn't mean we're at the mercy of our subconscious impulses. By learning to recognize and work with these deeper influences, we can cultivate greater autonomy in our thoughts and actions. Just as resilience can be strengthened through practice, so too can our relationship with the subconscious mind, using understanding and targeted exercises to foster greater harmony and self-awareness.

Accessing Subconscious Wisdom

The subconscious mind holds a vast repository of experiences, patterns, and insights that can enhance our decision-making and creativity. Research from Dr. Antonio Damasio's work at USC's Brain and Creativity Institute demonstrates how our subconscious processes integrate experience, emotion, and bodily signals to inform our choices and insights. His studies reveal that accessing this wisdom requires creating conditions where unconscious processing can effectively communicate with conscious awareness.

Several reliable methods have emerged from this research for accessing subconscious wisdom:

1. Body Awareness: Physical sensations often signal subconscious insights before conscious awareness catches up. That "gut feeling" about a situation or "weight on your shoulders" during stress represents your subconscious communicating through bodily sensations.

2. Dream Patterns: Our dreams can provide valuable windows into subconscious processing. Whether working through a challenging relationship or solving a complex problem, our dreams often reflect deeper patterns and potential solutions.

3. Creative Expression: Activities like free writing, drawing, or movement can bypass conscious censorship and allow subconscious insights to emerge. This explains why solutions to problems often appear when we're engaged in creative activities rather than direct problem solving.

4. Quiet Reflection: Periods of mental quiet, like those cultivated through mindfulness practice, allow subconscious insights to rise to conscious awareness. This is why breakthrough ideas often come during moments of relaxation rather than intense focus.

These methods work by creating conditions where the integration systems Dr. Damasio identified can function optimally, allowing unconscious wisdom to surface in ways we can recognize and apply. Understanding these pathways helps us cultivate a more productive relationship with our subconscious processes.

Working with Deep Patterns and Emotional Intelligence

Research from Dr. Joseph LeDoux at NYU's Center for Neural Science reveals how emotion and behavior intertwine in our subconscious processing. His studies demonstrate that our emotional brain systems operate faster and more automatically than conscious thought, profoundly influencing our behaviors before we're aware.

Understanding this rapid emotional processing helps explain why pure willpower often fails to create lasting change. When working to establish new habits or break old ones, success depends on aligning our conscious goals with subconscious emotional patterns. For instance, habit formation works best when we create environments and associations that resonate with our deeper emotional needs rather than relying solely on conscious determination.

The subconscious excels at processing emotional information, often recognizing subtle interpersonal signals and environmental cues before conscious awareness. LeDoux's research shows how these rapid emotional assessments shape our responses in challenging situations, from difficult conversations to critical decisions. Learning to recognize and work with these subconscious signals enhances both our emotional intelligence and our ability to navigate complex social situations.

Technology and Subconscious Awareness

Modern neuroscience tools offer new insights into these subconscious processes. Research from Stanford's Department of Psychiatry and Behavioral Sciences demonstrates how biofeedback and AI-enhanced monitoring can help us observe the physiological signals of subconscious activity. These tools can measure subtle changes in heart rate variability, skin conductance, and neural activity patterns that indicate subconscious processing at work. This technology allows us to recognize patterns we might otherwise miss and develop greater awareness of our automatic responses.

However, their findings emphasize that technology serves best as a bridge to self-awareness rather than a replacement for direct experience. The data these tools provide becomes meaningful only when integrated with our personal understanding and experience. For instance, while biofeedback might show us patterns in our stress response, the insights become truly valuable when we learn to recognize these patterns in real time without technological assistance.

This understanding connects directly to our earlier discussions of mindfulness and resilience. Just as those practices work best when technology enhances rather than replaces personal experience, our work with the subconscious mind benefits most from tools that support our natural capacity for self-understanding while maintaining the primacy of direct awareness. The goal is to use technology as a learning tool that eventually strengthens our natural ability to recognize and work with our subconscious processes.

Practical Applications: Working with Your Subconscious Mind

The following practices help you develop a stronger connection with your subconscious mind, building on the mindfulness, resilience, and creativity skills we've already explored. Each strategy creates bridges between your conscious intentions and subconscious patterns, leading to more integrated personal growth.

1. Morning Mind Mapping: Keep a journal by your bedside and capture your thoughts immediately upon waking. The transition between sleep and wakefulness offers unique access to subconscious material. Don't filter or edit, simply record whatever surfaces. Notice recurring themes, symbols, and patterns. This practice helps reveal the deeper currents influencing your daily choices and reactions.

2. Physical Signal Mapping: Set three daily check-in times to scan your body for physical sensations and emotional responses. Start from your feet and move upward, noting areas of tension, comfort, or emotional charge. These bodily sensations often reflect subconscious awareness before conscious recognition catches up. Track these patterns to recognize how your body signals important information before conscious awareness.

3. Decision Point Check-ins: Before making important decisions, pause to examine what's happening below the surface. Notice your physical sensations, emotional tone, and any subtle pushes or pulls you feel toward particular options. Document these responses to make subconscious patterns more visible. This practice

helps prevent unconscious biases from driving important choices.

4. Pattern Interruption: When you notice an unwanted habitual response, use conscious interruption to create space for new choices. If you habitually reach for your phone when feeling uncomfortable, pause and take three conscious breaths instead. This creates moments of conscious choice within automatic behaviors, gradually reshaping subconscious patterns.

5. Evening Integration: End each day with a brief review of significant moments, challenges, and insights. Notice which experiences carry an emotional charge or seem to want more attention. Write down any patterns you observe. This practice helps your conscious and subconscious minds process the day's experiences together.

6. Symbolic Expression: Use visual tools to explore and express subconscious themes. Create vision boards for future aspirations or draw/paint to process current challenges. Choose images and symbols that resonate emotionally rather than logically. This practice helps bypass conscious resistance and access deeper insights. Weekly sessions of 30 minutes allow for meaningful exploration while maintaining consistent practice.

7. Biofeedback Practice: Use technology like heart rate monitors, breathing apps, or stress tracking devices as learning tools. Observe how your physiological patterns shift during different mental and emotional states. Practice recognizing these physical signals without devices, using the

technology as training wheels for developing natural body awareness.

8. Movement Exploration: Set aside time for free form movement without predetermined patterns. Try different forms of unrestricted movement, dancing, stretching, or gentle swaying. Notice which movements feel restricted and which flow easily. This practice helps release subconscious patterns held in the body while revealing deeper emotional states.

9. Creative Dialogue: Establish regular conversations with different aspects of yourself through writing or art. Choose an issue you're working with and explore it from multiple inner perspectives, your practical side, your emotional self, your wisdom voice. This practice helps integrate different aspects of your psyche while accessing deeper insights.

10. Environmental Anchors: Shape your space with intentional cues that support desired patterns. Place meaningful objects, images, or words where you'll encounter them naturally throughout your day. Your subconscious mind continuously processes these environmental cues, even when you're not consciously aware of them, reinforcing positive subconscious patterns.

Begin with one or two practices that feel most natural and accessible to you. Remember that working with the subconscious mind is like learning a new language, it takes time, patience, and regular practice to develop fluency. Pay attention to what works best for you and adjust these practices to fit your personal style and schedule.

Remember that the goal isn't to control your subconscious mind but to develop a more cooperative relationship with it. Like the mindfulness practices we explored earlier, this work is about building awareness and understanding rather than forcing change. Through patient, consistent practice, you can create a more harmonious partnership between your conscious and subconscious minds, leading to more integrated and effective personal growth.

Chapter 6: Expanding Cultural and Philosophical Horizons

In our interconnected world, understanding and working with different perspectives and worldviews has become essential for personal growth and effective interaction with others. This expansion of our mental horizons adds new dimensions to our awareness and adaptability, enriching how we navigate both everyday situations and complex challenges.

Understanding Cultural Intelligence

Cultural intelligence, our ability to understand and navigate different worldviews, represents a fundamental human capacity that we can actively develop. Research from Dr. Soon Ang at Nanyang Technological University, a pioneer in cultural intelligence studies, demonstrates how this capability extends beyond knowledge of customs to encompass deeper understanding of diverse ways of thinking and being.

This capacity proves essential in our interconnected world. Whether collaborating on international projects, engaging with community initiatives, or participating in cross-cultural exchanges, cultural intelligence helps navigate complexity with greater wisdom and effectiveness.

Research reveals four interconnected dimensions of cultural intelligence:

1. Mindful Awareness: The ability to notice and suspend our automatic cultural assumptions, creating space for new understanding. For

instance, recognizing that your interpretation of "being on time" might differ from others, or noticing your immediate reactions to different communication styles in meetings or family gatherings.

2. Emotional Recognition: Understanding how emotions are expressed and interpreted differently across cultures and contexts. This might show up in recognizing that direct eye contact can signal respect in one setting but discomfort in another, or understanding that what appears as anger might actually be passionate engagement in a different cultural context.

3. Behavioral Flexibility: The capacity to adapt our approach while maintaining authenticity and personal integrity. Like adjusting your communication style when speaking with elderly relatives versus young children, or modifying your work presentation style for different audiences while staying true to your core message.

4. Learning Orientation: Maintaining genuine curiosity and openness to different perspectives and ways of being. This could mean actively seeking to understand why a neighbor's holiday celebrations differ from yours, or exploring why colleagues from different backgrounds approach problem solving in unique ways.

Dr. Ang's research emphasizes that developing these capacities isn't about abandoning our own cultural foundation but expanding our ability to understand and connect with others. Like learning a new language, we add new ways of understanding and expressing ourselves while maintaining our core identity.

Wisdom Traditions in Modern Life

Research in comparative philosophy and cultural anthropology reveals how ancient wisdom traditions offer sophisticated frameworks for modern challenges. These approaches provide tested strategies for navigating complexity, uncertainty, and change.

Stoic philosophy offers particularly relevant tools for our digital age. Beyond distinguishing between controllable and uncontrollable factors, Stoic practices teach emotional regulation through rational analysis and perspective taking. In professional settings, this manifests as focusing energy on process improvement rather than market speculation. In personal life, it helps prioritize meaningful interactions over digital distraction.

Buddhist psychology provides complementary insights through concepts like impermanence and non-attachment. These principles help navigate technological disruption, career transitions, and relationship changes. For instance, understanding impermanence helps professionals view industry evolution as natural rather than threatening, while non-attachment principles guide balanced engagement with social media and digital connectivity.

Indigenous wisdom traditions contribute vital perspectives on systemic thinking and ecological awareness. The understanding of interconnectedness informs modern sustainability practices, from urban planning to corporate responsibility. More importantly, indigenous approaches to community building, emphasizing reciprocity, shared responsibility, and intergenerational learning, offer proven models for strengthening social bonds in our increasingly fragmented society.

These traditions work together synergistically. Stoic emotional regulation combines with Buddhist acceptance to build resilience, while indigenous community practices enhance both through collective support systems. Modern neuroscience and psychology continue to validate many of these traditional insights, while new applications emerge for contemporary challenges. This integration of ancient wisdom with modern understanding creates robust frameworks for personal and collective growth.

Modern Applications of Traditional Wisdom

Traditional wisdom offers practical tools for modern challenges when thoughtfully adapted. The Harvard Divinity School's research on contemplative practices demonstrates how ancient approaches can address contemporary issues like digital overwhelm and work-life complexity.

Different traditions provide complementary approaches to modern challenges. Stoic philosophy's emphasis on examining our reactions rather than external circumstances offers a powerful framework for managing digital stress. Instead of fighting against information overload, we learn to understand and adjust our responses to it. This approach helps transform social media from a source of anxiety to a tool we can engage with mindfully.

Eastern philosophical approaches to balance and harmony provide insights for modern work-life integration. The Taoist concept of dynamic equilibrium, for instance, suggests viewing balance not as a fixed state but as a continuous process of adjustment. This perspective transforms the challenge of managing competing demands from a source of stress into an opportunity for developing adaptability.

Bridging Different Worldviews

Research from the MIT Comparative Media Studies program shows that the ability to bridge different perspectives and find common ground has become a crucial skill in our interconnected world. Their studies demonstrate that effective bridging isn't about adopting every viewpoint, but developing the capacity to understand and work with different ways of thinking.

This bridging capability creates value across contexts, helping families connect across generational differences, facilitating community dialogue about development, and enabling teams to transform diverse perspectives into innovative solutions.

Cross-cultural research has identified key principles for bridging different worldviews:

1. Start Where You Are: Begin by examining your own cultural assumptions and biases. This self-awareness creates a foundation for understanding others. For example, a healthcare provider might first recognize their own assumptions about healing before engaging with different cultural approaches to medicine.

2. Seek Understanding Before Judgment: Explore the context and reasoning behind unfamiliar practices. When encountering different approaches to education, for instance, investigate the values and goals driving these methods rather than evaluating them against familiar standards.

3. Focus on Common Ground: Before addressing differences, identify underlying shared values and goals. In community conflicts, finding mutual priorities, like public safety or child welfare, creates a foundation for productive dialogue about differing approaches.

4. Practice Humble Curiosity: Approach differences with genuine interest and openness to learning. Rather than categorizing unfamiliar practices as right or wrong, explore how they serve their context and what insights they might offer.

These bridging principles work together to create deeper understanding across differences. When we combine self-awareness with genuine curiosity, and seek understanding before making judgments, we develop the capacity to find shared ground even in seemingly opposing viewpoints. This skill becomes increasingly valuable as our world grows more interconnected, enabling us to transform diversity from a potential source of conflict into a catalyst for innovation and growth.

Technology and Collective Growth

Research from MIT's Digital Anthropology Lab demonstrates how digital platforms can enhance cultural understanding when used intentionally. Virtual environments enable direct engagement with different cultural practices and philosophical approaches, from learning traditional cooking methods to studying meditation with teachers worldwide. However, these tools prove most valuable when they complement rather than replace in person interactions.

The challenge lies in using technology to expand rather than reinforce existing perspectives. Studies from the Pew Research Center show that digital platforms can either broaden cultural exposure or strengthen existing biases, depending on how we engage with them. Success requires bringing the same openness and discernment to digital interactions that we cultivate in face-to-face encounters.

This expanded cultural awareness creates ripple effects throughout communities. Research from Harvard's Project Zero demonstrates how individual growth in cultural understanding transforms broader social networks. Organizations become more innovative when embracing diverse perspectives. Communities grow more resilient through strengthened connections between different groups. Educational institutions better serve their populations by understanding and working with varied cultural approaches.

These changes often begin small but gain momentum through social networks. One person's effort to understand different perspectives inspires others to expand their worldview. Teams practicing inclusive decision-making influence entire organizational cultures. This collective growth transforms differences from potential barriers into sources of community strength and innovation.

Practical Applications: Expanding Cultural and Philosophical Horizons

The following practices are designed to help you develop deeper understanding across cultural and philosophical differences while enhancing your ability to navigate diverse perspectives in daily life. Each strategy offers practical ways to expand your horizons while maintaining your authentic center.

1. Create Cultural Learning Moments: Transform daily encounters into opportunities for understanding. When you encounter different approaches to common situations, whether it's how a colleague organizes their work or how a neighbor celebrates holidays, pause to understand rather than judge. Notice your initial reactions and get curious about the wisdom behind unfamiliar practices.

2. Engage in Cultural Exchange: Create meaningful opportunities for cultural learning across multiple formats. Balance digital platforms like cultural exchange forums with in-person community gatherings. Structure these exchanges around shared activities and storytelling, allowing diverse perspectives to emerge naturally through authentic interaction.

3. Develop Bridging Communication: Practice adapting your communication to different cultural contexts while maintaining authenticity. Start by identifying shared values and common ground, then build understanding through careful listening and thoughtful expression. Notice how different audiences require different approaches while keeping core meanings intact.

4. Build Learning Partnerships: Establish ongoing exchange relationships with people from different backgrounds. Create regular opportunities for mutual learning through language exchange, skill sharing, or cultural discussion. Focus on developing deep, lasting connections that support genuine cultural understanding.

5. Apply Wisdom Traditions: Integrate principles from different philosophical and cultural traditions into your daily life. Experiment with combining approaches, like Stoic emotional regulation with Buddhist acceptance, or indigenous community practices with modern collaboration. Document how these combinations enhance your approach to modern challenges.

6. Practice Mindful Cultural Learning: Develop reflection practices that help you process cross-cultural experiences while maintaining personal boundaries. Regular journaling and self-check-ins help distinguish between expanding your perspective and losing your center. This balanced approach supports authentic growth while preserving integrity.

7. Create Inclusive Environments: Design spaces and interactions that welcome diverse perspectives while supporting meaningful exchange. Whether in professional or personal settings, consider how physical setup, communication patterns, and group dynamics can better support varied cultural expressions and ways of thinking.

8. Develop Cultural Intelligence: Actively build your capacity to navigate cultural differences through

systematic practice. Start with understanding your own cultural assumptions, then progressively engage with increasingly unfamiliar perspectives and practices. Notice how your comfort with difference grows through consistent exposure and reflection.

9. Foster Reciprocal Learning: Create opportunities for mutual exchange where all participants both teach and learn. Structure interactions so different cultural perspectives receive equal consideration and respect. This approach builds deeper understanding while strengthening community bonds.

10. Cross-Cultural Problem-Solving Practice: When facing challenges, consciously explore insights from different cultural frameworks. Consider how various traditions might approach the situation, then thoughtfully integrate these perspectives into innovative solutions. Document how different approaches complement each other and lead to more comprehensive outcomes.

Begin with practices that feel most natural and accessible in your current situation. You might start with simple perspective taking exercises in daily life before organizing larger cultural exchange events. Developing cultural understanding is a gradual process that is built through consistent, thoughtful practice. As you practice these approaches, notice how your capacity for understanding grows naturally over time. What once seemed foreign or challenging might become interesting or enlightening. This gradual expansion of perspective creates a stronger foundation for navigating our increasingly interconnected world with wisdom and grace.

Remember, the goal isn't to become an expert in every tradition or to adopt every perspective you encounter. Rather, it's about developing the capacity to understand, appreciate, and work effectively with different viewpoints while maintaining your own authentic path. This expanded awareness enriches your life while contributing to more meaningful connections in your family, workplace, and community.

Chapter 7: Mastering Modern Complexity

We face complexity every day, whether managing family dynamics, navigating career changes, or contributing to our communities. Understanding how complex situations differ from merely complicated ones gives us better tools for handling these challenges. While a complicated task, like following a detailed recipe, requires careful attention to specific steps, complex situations – like raising a child or building team harmony – involve countless interconnected factors that can't be reduced to simple formulas.

Understanding Complex Challenges

Dr. David Snowden's *Cynefin* framework shows us there's a crucial difference between complex and complicated situations. Think of it this way: complicated challenges are like following a recipe, they might have many steps, but the steps are known and the results predictable. Complex challenges are more like growing a garden, you can create good conditions for growth, but you can't control exactly how things will develop.

Understanding this difference changes how we tackle challenges. Building strong relationships, developing team culture, or supporting community growth all involve elements that interact and evolve in ways we can't fully predict or control. Success comes from understanding and working with these natural patterns rather than trying to control every detail.

Research in complexity science has identified several key features that characterize complex situations:

1. Interconnectedness: Multiple factors influence each other in ways that aren't always obvious at first. Like a web where pulling one thread causes movement throughout the system, changes ripple in unpredictable ways that defy simple cause-and-effect analysis.

2. Emergence: New patterns arise naturally from countless small interactions, often surprising us. Group dynamics evolve in unexpected ways through daily exchanges rather than direct control, creating outcomes we couldn't predict by looking at individual parts.

3. Adaptation: Situations change as we interact with them, like a conversation that evolves as ideas emerge. Each intervention creates new conditions that require us to adjust our approach, making continuous adjustment part of the process.

4. Multiple Perspectives: Different people experience and understand the same situation in unique ways, like how everyone at a shared meal might experience the same dish differently based on their tastes and preferences. These diverse viewpoints enrich our understanding and shape how situations develop.

Understanding these patterns helps us work more effectively with complex situations. Rather than trying to control every detail, we can focus on recognizing patterns and supporting positive developments as they naturally emerge.

Integrative Thinking in Complex Situations

When facing complex challenges, traditional either/or thinking often falls short. Research from the Rotman School of Management demonstrates how this limited perspective overlooks creative possibilities. By studying how successful leaders approach complex problems, researchers found that the ability to integrate opposing ideas, rather than choosing between them, leads to more innovative and sustainable solutions.

This approach transforms how we handle common tensions in modern life. Consider the challenge of technology use, many feel caught between limiting screen time and embracing digital opportunities. Integrative thinking reveals another path, creating environments that combine clear boundaries with meaningful engagement. This might involve designing structured times for different types of activities, using technology as a tool for learning and creativity while maintaining space for direct human connection.

The same principle demonstrates how integrative thinking transforms apparent contradictions into opportunities. Rather than seeing structure and innovation as opposing forces, we can design frameworks where established processes create the safety needed for exploration. Clear guidelines and systematic feedback help new ideas develop while maintaining necessary stability, showing how integrated solutions often surpass either/or choices.

Systems Awareness in Daily Life

Complex situations require us to see the bigger picture, how different elements influence each other in ongoing ways. Dr. Donella Meadows' research on systems thinking demonstrated that small, well-placed actions can create significant positive changes throughout a system when we understand how elements interconnect.

Systems thinking transforms our approach to common challenges. Consider how behaviors and habits influence each other: sleep quality affects food choices, which impacts energy levels, which influences daily activity, which shapes sleep patterns. Understanding these feedback loops helps identify effective starting points for change, where small adjustments create ripple effects throughout the entire system.

This understanding applies equally to larger challenges. A community initiative viewed through systems awareness reveals how different elements support each other: shared spaces foster connections, which build trust, which encourages participation, which strengthens the community fabric. Rather than tackling issues in isolation, this approach leads to solutions that address multiple needs simultaneously, creating positive cycles of improvement.

Building Adaptive Capacity

In our rapidly evolving world, the ability to adapt becomes increasingly crucial. Traditional approaches to handling change focus on planning and prediction, but modern challenges, from AI integration to shifting work patterns, require us to develop a more dynamic capability. We need to build our capacity to learn, adjust, and thrive amid constant transformation.

This mental agility differs from simple flexibility. It involves developing specific capabilities that help us work effectively with emerging technologies and evolving systems. When artificial intelligence transforms industry practices, when digital platforms reshape communication patterns, or when new tools change how we work, success depends not on mastering any particular change, but on building our ability to adapt continuously.

Developing this capacity involves several key elements:

1. Active Learning: Cultivating the ability to learn quickly from new situations through experimentation with emerging technologies, exploration of different approaches to digital collaboration, and discovery of new ways to balance connectivity with focus.

2. Pattern Recognition: Developing the ability to identify meaningful trends and relationships in complex situations, distinguishing between temporary disruptions and significant shifts that require adaptation.

3. Experimental Mindset: Building comfort with testing new approaches thoughtfully, exploring possibilities while managing potential risks rather than simply embracing or resisting change.

4. Systematic Reflection: Establishing regular practices for assessing what works and what doesn't, converting experience into insight for handling future changes more effectively.

This adaptive capacity serves us across modern challenges. Whether integrating new technologies into our workflow, navigating changing organizational structures, or developing new skills for emerging opportunities, we build our ability to engage productively with change rather than being overwhelmed by it.

Emotional Intelligence in Complex Systems

Navigating complexity requires more than analytical skills, it demands emotional intelligence. Dr. Daniel Goleman's research at Harvard has demonstrated how emotional intelligence becomes crucial in complex situations where multiple stakeholders bring different needs and perspectives. His work shows that success in such environments depends heavily on our ability to recognize, understand, and work with both our own emotions and those of others.

This capability becomes increasingly vital as our systems grow more complex and interconnected. When organizations implement new technologies, teams work across digital platforms, or communities face significant change, the emotional dimension often determines success or failure. Understanding emotional patterns helps us recognize resistance, spot opportunities, and guide positive development in these complex environments.

Consider how this works in practice. When adopting new ways of communicating, whether through video calls or collaboration tools, the challenge extends beyond learning the technology. The real complexity emerges in the human response, concerns about maintaining authentic connection, hopes for better ways to work together, worries about losing the warmth of in-person interaction. These feelings shape how people engage with and adopt new tools. By understanding and working with these emotional responses rather than focusing only on technical training, we create solutions that work better for everyone involved.

This emotional awareness transforms how we handle complexity. Rather than seeing emotions as obstacles to rational decision-making, we recognize them as essential signals that reveal underlying patterns and possibilities. This integration of emotional and analytical understanding helps us develop more effective and sustainable solutions for modern challenges.

Technology and Complexity

Modern technology offers powerful tools for understanding and working with complex systems, while also adding new layers of complexity to navigate. Success comes not from relying solely on technological solutions, but from learning to integrate digital capabilities with human insight, using technology to enhance rather than replace our natural abilities to understand and work with complex situations.

Different tools serve distinct purposes in helping us navigate complexity. Visualization platforms help us see patterns and relationships that might otherwise remain hidden. AI-powered analysis reveals connections in large amounts of information. Collaboration tools enable us to work across boundaries of time and space. Yet real value emerges when we combine these capabilities thoughtfully with human understanding and experience.

This integration appears in daily navigation of modern life. While apps can track our tasks, schedules, and connections, successful coordination depends on understanding personal rhythms and relationships. Digital learning platforms can analyze study patterns, but meaningful development requires recognizing individual learning styles and motivations. Even smart home systems can automate routines, but creating comfortable living spaces demands understanding how people actually move through and use their environments.

The key lies in developing our capacity to work with technology as a complement to human capability. Rather than becoming dependent on digital tools or avoiding them entirely, we can learn to combine technological advantages with human wisdom. This balanced approach helps us navigate complexity more effectively, using digital capabilities to enhance our understanding while maintaining human insight as the guiding force.

Collective Intelligence and Complex Challenges

Complex situations require more knowledge and perspective than any individual can possess. Dr. Geoff Mulgan's research at University College London's Institute for Innovation and Public Purpose demonstrates how collective intelligence emerges through structured collaboration. His work shows that successful collective problem solving depends not just on gathering diverse perspectives, but on creating systems that effectively integrate and apply shared knowledge.

Creating these conditions requires thoughtful design. While digital platforms enable broader participation, successful collaboration depends on how effectively these tools structure interaction and decision-making. For instance, when communities address shared challenges, the most successful approaches combine accessible participation methods with clear processes for synthesizing insights and implementing solutions. This might involve using digital platforms to gather initial ideas, facilitating structured discussions to develop these concepts, and creating clear pathways for moving from insight to action.

Modern collaboration tools have expanded possibilities for collective intelligence. Asynchronous communication platforms, shared workspaces, and collaborative decision-making tools enable groups to work together across time zones and distances. However, research shows that technology alone doesn't ensure effective collaboration. Success requires balancing technological capabilities with human facilitation, ensuring that tools support rather than substitute for meaningful interaction and careful consideration of diverse perspectives.

Practical Applications: Navigating Complex Challenges

The following strategies help you develop the capabilities needed to work effectively with complexity in our modern world. Each practice builds upon and complements the others, strengthening your capacity to understand and navigate complex challenges while maintaining clarity and purpose. Together, they create a practical framework for applying the principles we've explored throughout this chapter.

1. Develop Pattern Recognition: Start noticing how different elements of complex situations influence each other in both digital and physical spaces. Observe how changes ripple through systems, whether in team dynamics, family relationships, or community networks. Document the patterns you notice, looking for recurring themes and connections that reveal the system's natural behavior.

2. Create Learning Cycles: Establish regular practices for experimenting, reflecting, and adjusting your approaches. Start small, test new methods thoughtfully, and take time to understand what works and why. Use digital tools and personal reflection to track insights, building your understanding of how complex situations respond to different interventions.

3. Map Multiple Perspectives: When facing complex challenges, explore how different participants experience and understand the situation. Consider both practical viewpoints and emotional responses, building a rich picture of hopes, concerns, and underlying needs. This layered understanding reveals natural pathways toward integrated solutions.

4. Design Thoughtful Experiments: Create safe ways to test new approaches without risking major disruption. Whether trying new collaboration methods, communication practices, or technological tools, structure your experiments to maximize learning while managing potential risks. Document both successes and setbacks to build your understanding.

5. Build Diverse Networks: Cultivate relationships with people who bring different perspectives, experiences, and expertise to complex challenges. Include both in-person and digital connections, creating a rich network that enhances your understanding and approach. Regular dialogue across these networks helps reveal patterns and possibilities you might otherwise miss.

6. Practice Systems Awareness: Before attempting solutions, invest time in understanding how the current system operates. Notice existing patterns, natural rhythms, and potential leverage points. Observe both human dynamics and technological factors, looking for ways they interact and influence each other. This understanding helps you work with rather than against the system's natural tendencies.

7. Create Integration Environments: Develop spaces and practices that support working with complexity. This might mean establishing regular times for collaborative problem-solving, using digital platforms effectively for group learning, or creating quiet spaces for personal reflection. These environments help maintain focus while encouraging creative approaches to complex challenges.

8. Develop Adaptive Planning: Rather than trying to predict exact outcomes, build your capacity to anticipate and respond to change. Consider multiple possible futures, identify early warning signs, and prepare flexible responses. This approach helps you remain both proactive and adaptable in facing emerging challenges.

9. Cultivate Emotional Intelligence: Develop your capacity to recognize and work with emotional patterns in complex situations. Practice noticing emotional currents in both in-person and digital interactions, understanding how feelings influence behavior and decisions. Use this awareness to create more effective and sustainable solutions.

10. Maintain Sustainable Engagement: While building these capabilities, establish practices that support your ongoing development. Balance active engagement with reflection time, technological connection with human interaction, and challenge with recovery. This equilibrium allows you to work effectively with complexity while continuing to grow and learn.

Begin with practices that align naturally with your current situation and needs. Start small, establish consistency, and gradually expand your approach. Remember that developing these capabilities is itself a complex process that unfolds over time through patient, persistent practice.

The goal isn't to eliminate complexity but to build your capacity to work effectively within it. As you develop these practices, you'll find yourself better equipped to navigate complex challenges while contributing to positive outcomes in both personal and professional contexts.

Chapter 8: Sustaining Lifelong Growth and Adaptation

Personal growth and adaptation aren't one-time achievements but ongoing processes that unfold throughout our lives. In our rapidly evolving world, where technology constantly reshapes how we work and connect, the ability to sustain meaningful development becomes increasingly crucial. Understanding how to keep learning, growing, and adapting, while maintaining balance and authenticity, creates the foundation for long-term success and fulfillment. This journey requires both time-tested wisdom about how we develop and fresh insights about thriving amid accelerating change.

Understanding Long-Term Change

The science of lasting change reveals how we can develop sustainably over time. Research from Dr. Richard Davidson at the University of Wisconsin-Madison's Center for Healthy Minds shows that meaningful development depends on understanding how our brains encode and integrate new learning.

Several key principles emerge from this research:

1. Focused Intensity: Deep engagement creates stronger changes than passive exposure. When we give full attention to mastering a new skill or understanding a new concept, even brief sessions create meaningful progress. Like developing a new habit, each focused practice builds stronger neural pathways than hours of casual attention.

2. Recovery Integration: Our brains need time to process and consolidate new learning. Building regular reflection periods into our development, whether after learning sessions or at day's end, allows new understanding to settle and strengthen. This balance of engagement and integration supports lasting change.

3. Emotional Resonance: Changes stick when they connect with personal meaning. Understanding how a new capability enhances our goals and values transforms it from abstract knowledge into meaningful development. This connection helps new learning become part of our natural way of operating.

4. Varied Application: New skills become more robust through diverse practice. Applying new approaches across different situations, from professional challenges to personal growth, builds flexible, adaptable capabilities. This variety helps learning transfer naturally to new contexts.

5. Progressive Challenge: Growth happens at the edge of our comfort zone. Starting with manageable steps and gradually increasing complexity builds confidence while maintaining engagement. This measured progression creates sustainable development without overwhelming our capacity for change.

These principles work together in a dynamic relationship, each supporting and amplifying the others. When we align our development practices with these natural patterns of learning and growth, change becomes more sustainable and meaningful. Like other complex systems we've explored, lasting development emerges not from forcing change, but from creating conditions where growth naturally flourishes.

Building Sustainable Practices

Research in behavioral science offers valuable insights about creating lasting changes in our modern world. Dr. BJ Fogg's work demonstrates that sustainable behavior changes do not come from relying on motivation or willpower, but from designing small, easy-to-adopt actions and understanding how new behaviors naturally take root and grow through prompts and incremental progress.

One particularly powerful approach involves connecting new practices to our existing routines. This strategy recognizes that we already have stable patterns woven throughout our day, both in our physical and digital lives. By thoughtfully attaching new behaviors to these established routines, we create natural triggers for growth. The coffee that starts our day becomes a cue for brief reflection. The login screen that greets us becomes a reminder to set clear intentions. The walk to lunch offers space for learning review.

These connections work naturally because they build on patterns already embedded in our daily flow. As we start small and notice what works best, these linked practices grow stronger and adapt with our changing routines. Each successful connection builds confidence for the next step, allowing us to gradually expand our practice while maintaining stability.

This foundation of reliable practices supports long-term development. As our capabilities grow, we can adjust the complexity and scope of our practices. What starts as a brief morning reflection might evolve into a deeper learning practice. A simple intention-setting moment could develop into more sophisticated planning. This natural evolution helps us maintain steady progress while continuing to challenge our growth.

Creating Growth Ecosystems

Meaningful development depends on the environments and systems we build around our learning. Dr. Angela Duckworth's work at the University of Pennsylvania demonstrates that lasting growth emerges not just from personal effort, but from creating systems that naturally encourage progress in our rapidly evolving world. Like a well-tended garden, our development needs conditions that adapt and grow with us.

Growth ecosystems emerge naturally in our daily spaces. Thoughtful arrangement of our environments, whether physical or digital, can significantly reduce friction and invite engagement. Simple adjustments to our surroundings create natural opportunities for learning and development. Each space, designed with intention, supports different aspects of growth and adapts as our needs change.

Social connections form another vital part of these ecosystems. Mentors provide guidance and challenge our thinking. Peers share experiences and offer fresh perspectives. Learning communities create natural accountability while offering support. These relationships evolve across both in-person and digital interactions, creating dynamic networks that grow with us.

Resources complement these foundations, organized to support ongoing development. Tools and materials, both physical and digital, remain accessible, and update as technology advances. Learning spaces flex to accommodate new ways of working and learning. This adaptable arrangement helps maintain momentum through changing circumstances and emerging challenges.

The power of growth ecosystems lies in their ability to evolve while supporting stable progress. As our needs change and new technologies emerge, these systems adapt naturally. Physical spaces transform to support new ways of connecting. Social networks expand across platforms. Resources update to embrace new possibilities. When thoughtfully designed, these dynamic systems support sustainable development in our constantly changing world.

Technology as a Growth Partner

Modern technology offers unprecedented tools for supporting sustained development yet requires thoughtful integration. Research from MIT's Media Lab demonstrates that technology provides the most value when it enhances rather than replaces natural learning processes. Success comes from choosing tools that support development while preserving our autonomy in the growth process.

The emergence of AI-enhanced learning platforms illustrates this balance. These systems can track patterns in your development, suggest optimal practice times, and adapt to your learning style. However, research shows they work best when supporting rather than directing growth. For instance, while AI can analyze music practice patterns and suggest improvements, the artist's personal connection to their craft remains essential. Similarly, language learning apps work most effectively when combined with real conversation practice.

Digital tools for habit tracking and skill development have evolved to offer sophisticated support. While apps can provide personalized reminders, visualize progress patterns, and connect us with supportive communities, studies from Stanford's Human-Computer Interaction Lab show they work best when thoughtfully integrated into our development strategies. Using these tools intentionally helps enhance our natural growth processes while preserving the human elements essential for meaningful progress.

Navigating Future Challenges

As we look ahead, the ability to sustain growth becomes increasingly crucial. Dr. David Eagleman's research at Stanford demonstrates how advances in neuroscience and technology create new possibilities for development. His work shows that while specific technological skills evolve rapidly, our fundamental capacity for learning and adaptation grows more valuable.

In this landscape of accelerating change, success depends less on mastering tools and more on developing core capabilities that support continuous growth. Several key approaches help navigate this evolution:

1. Adaptive Learning: Develop the ability to learn and relearn as circumstances change. Regularly explore new fields while finding fresh perspectives on familiar knowledge. This flexibility helps maintain relevance while building deeper understanding.

2. Balanced Integration: Create sustainable ways to incorporate new tools and practices. Choose technologies that enhance natural learning patterns rather than complicate development. Focus on innovations that support rather than strain growth.

3. Community Connection: Build diverse networks that provide both stability and innovation. Balance relationships with early adopters who inspire new possibilities and experienced practitioners who offer grounding wisdom. These varied perspectives help navigate change while maintaining continuity.

4. Development Pacing: Establish rhythms that support steady progress without overwhelm. Alternate periods of intensive learning with time for integration. This balanced approach helps maintain momentum through changing circumstances.

5. Ethical Awareness: Consider how personal development affects broader systems. Understand the ripple effects of growth choices on communities and future possibilities. This perspective helps ensure development serves both individual and collective progress.

These complementary approaches create a foundation for ongoing growth. By developing fundamental capacities for learning and adaptation while maintaining strong support systems, we can embrace new opportunities while preserving essential human elements. This prepares us to thrive amid increasing complexity and change.

Practical Applications: Sustaining Growth and Development

The following strategies help create sustainable approaches to long-term growth and adaptation. Each practice builds your capacity for ongoing development while maintaining balance and momentum. While some approaches might resonate more strongly than others, together they create a robust foundation for lifelong learning and evolution.

1. Design Learning Environments: Set up spaces that make growth natural and easy. Create a physical workspace that invites focus and learning, like a reading corner with good light or a clutter-free desk. Organize digital tools to support rather than distract. Connect with mentors who guide you, peers who share your journey, and communities that offer new perspectives. These thoughtful arrangements help make development a natural part of your daily life.

2. Create Growth Checkpoints: Set up regular times to review your development journey. Start each morning by noting what you want to learn, use the commute home to reflect on key insights, and take time each weekend to consider bigger patterns. Keep track of specific examples, what you tried, what worked well, what you might adjust. This systematic attention helps you spot opportunities and maintain momentum.

3. Build Recovery Rhythms: Design deliberate pauses in your learning schedule. Create morning quiet time before diving into work, take actual breaks between focused sessions, and protect evening hours for processing. Use these periods

for activities that help your mind integrate, whether walking, gentle movement, or simply sitting quietly. These intentional breaks help turn information into understanding.

4. Nurture Learning Relationships: Develop connections that enrich different aspects of growth. Schedule monthly conversations with someone whose work inspires you, join regular skill-sharing sessions with peers, and participate in groups that stretch your thinking. Set clear intentions for these relationships, what you hope to learn, how you can contribute, when you'll connect. These structured interactions create natural support for development.

5. Strengthen New Learning: Create specific practices for deepening understanding. After learning sessions, take 10 minutes to write key points in your own words. During daily activities, notice how new concepts connect to what you're doing. Share one important insight each week with someone who can offer fresh perspective. This active engagement helps knowledge become practical wisdom.

6. Join Learning Communities: Build meaningful connections around shared growth. Find groups that match your interests, whether online forums, local meetups, or professional networks. Participate regularly, share your experiences, ask thoughtful questions, offer support to others. Schedule time each week to engage, making community learning a natural part of your routine.

7. Apply Across Domains: Practice using insights in different contexts. When you learn something at

work, consider how it might improve home life. When you discover helpful personal practices, explore how they could enhance professional projects. Keep notes about these connections and experiment with different combinations. This deliberate cross-pollination creates deeper understanding and practical value.

8. Find Natural Rhythms: Develop patterns that match your natural energy flow. Notice when you learn best, perhaps early mornings for deep work, afternoons for collaborative projects, evenings for reflection. Plan challenging learning for high-energy times, leaving routine tasks for when focus naturally dips. This alignment helps maintain steady progress while preserving energy.

9. Stay Adaptable: Create structure that supports flexibility. Set quarterly learning goals but review them monthly, adjusting as new opportunities emerge. Keep a running list of interests to explore when timing feels right. Regular check-ins help your development path evolve naturally while maintaining clear direction.

10. Balance Digital Tools: Choose technology that truly serves your growth. Set up your phone to show learning resources before social media, use apps that track progress without becoming a burden, create digital spaces that encourage focus. Schedule regular reviews of your tools, keeping what enhances learning, removing what distracts. This thoughtful integration lets technology support rather than direct your development.

Begin with strategies that align most closely with your current growth goals and lifestyle. Start small, establish consistency with one or two practices, then gradually add more as these become habitual. Remember that sustainable growth comes from finding approaches that you can maintain over the long term. Trust your intuition about what serves your development while remaining open to new methods and perspectives.

The journey of sustained growth isn't about constant striving or endless self-improvement. Instead, it's about creating rhythms and practices that support your natural development while maintaining balance and well-being. Some periods will involve intense learning and change, while others focus more on integration and consolidation. Both are essential parts of the growth cycle.

Remember that sustainable development emerges through consistent attention rather than sporadic effort. Small, regular practices often create more lasting change than occasional intense pushes. By approaching your growth journey with patience and persistence, you create conditions for ongoing development that can adapt and evolve with you throughout life.

Conclusion: The Ever-Evolving Journey

As we conclude this exploration of mindset development, we find ourselves equipped with both understanding and practical tools for growth. The journey ahead isn't about reaching a final destination but about applying these insights to create meaningful change in our lives, our relationships, and our communities.

Throughout this book, we've discovered how research illuminates the brain's remarkable capacity for change, while traditional wisdom offers tested approaches for personal development. These elements work together in a profound dance of mutual enhancement. Mindfulness builds the foundation for resilience, helping you stay centered during challenges, while that same resilience gives you the confidence to explore your creativity more freely. As your creative capacity expands, you discover new approaches to change, strengthening your adaptability. Your growing understanding of complexity deepens your mindful awareness by revealing the subtle interconnections in your life, while cultural intelligence opens new creative horizons by offering fresh perspectives. Working with the subconscious mind acts as a powerful catalyst, deepening and enriching all these capabilities as they develop and interweave.

Yet perhaps our most crucial insight is this: in today's rapidly evolving world, consciously developing our mindset isn't just beneficial, it's essential. The challenges we face in our families, workplaces, and communities require new ways of thinking, learning, and being. The approaches we've explored aren't theoretical concepts but practical tools for navigating modern life with greater wisdom and effectiveness.

The journey of personal growth requires us to navigate important balances in our daily lives. We learn to leverage technology while maintaining our human connections, to embrace change while staying grounded in our values, to pursue individual development while contributing to our communities. We discover how to blend traditional wisdom with modern innovation, and how to combine structured practice with organic growth.

These balances play out in countless daily moments. When we use mindfulness to remain present while managing digital demands. When we apply resilience practices during organizational change. When we explore creative solutions to community challenges while honoring diverse perspectives. Each situation offers opportunities to apply and refine these capabilities.

Remember that sustainable growth emerges through consistent, mindful evolution rather than dramatic transformations. Small, regular practices, a few minutes of morning reflection, a thoughtful pause before important conversations, a brief evening review of lessons learned, gradually create profound change. The practices we've explored aren't meant to be perfected but to serve as reliable companions on your journey.

Ancient wisdom teaches us that change is constant, and we too are constantly evolving. This understanding resonates deeply in our time. Each day brings new situations that invite us to apply and expand our capabilities, to integrate new technologies thoughtfully, and to navigate emerging complexities with greater skill.

Your path forward will be uniquely yours. The frameworks and practices shared here aren't rigid prescriptions but adaptable guidelines to shape according to your circumstances and aspirations. Trust in your capacity for growth while maintaining patience with the process. Celebrate progress while staying curious about new possibilities.

The integration of science, technology, and traditional wisdom offers unprecedented opportunities for human development. Yet amidst these possibilities for transformation, remember that the goal isn't perfection, it's progress. It's about becoming more aware, more adaptable, and more alive to the opportunities each moment brings for learning and growth.

May this book serve as a trusted companion on your journey of discovery and development. The practices you've learned and insights you've gained are seeds planted in the garden of your future self. Nurture them with patience and persistence, remaining open to unexpected growth and new understanding. Your journey of mindset development is a lifelong adventure that becomes richer and more rewarding with each step forward.

The future is unwritten, and your capacity for development is boundless. The question isn't whether you can grow and adapt, but how you'll choose to shape your evolution in the years ahead. What possibilities will you explore? What challenges will you transform into opportunities? What contributions will you make to the lives of others?

Your next chapter begins now.

About The Author

Life's challenges have taught me that balance isn't something we find, it's something we create, one intentional step at a time. Through loss, profound change, and raw human experience I've learned that our deepest growth often comes from our hardest moments. These experiences showed me that transformation happens not by escaping life's complexities, but by meeting them with curiosity and courage.

Mindset Evolution emerged from combining research-based strategies with real-world experience, creating a practical framework for navigating our modern world. This book is an invitation to develop resilience, clarity, and purpose, not by avoiding challenges, but by transforming them into opportunities for growth.

May these pages inspire you to approach each day with intention, becoming stronger than yesterday and braver for tomorrow.

Your Voice Matters!

Thank you for embarking on the journey of ***Mindset Evolution***.

If this book sparked insight, challenged your thinking, or supported you in any way, I'd be so grateful if you took a moment to share your experience.

Leave Feedback

Your honest feedback helps me grow, and helps shape future resources. Whether it's a quick thought, a favorite takeaway, or something you'd love to see next, I'd love to hear from you.

Leave a Review on Amazon

Reviews help this book reach more people, and make a real difference in spreading the message of mindful, empowered growth.

Thank you again for reading, reflecting, and growing alongside me.

www.ingramcontent.com/pod-product-compliance
Lightning Source LLC
Chambersburg PA
CBHW031430210526
45464CB00005B/2135